What People Think of
Cultivating Perennial Churches

"Bob Dale has created a new and needed phrase for those of us invested in the future of the local church. *Cultivating Perennial Churches* vividly describes the kind of church any pastor would love to serve. Bob's engaging metaphor holds up as he unfolds a strategic model for church health and growth that mirrors the beautiful truths of the plant world. As a fan of perennials in my yard, I found myself convinced that perennial churches represent our best hope for God's kingdom in the twenty-first century. Using approachable and realistic churches as case studies, he vividly illustrates how his synthesis of experiences and sound theology combine to provide principles that make sense in the real world garden of local church life. Truly a 'must-read' for those trying to grow a church that will last."

BILL WILSON, pastor, First Baptist Church, Dalton, Georgia

"Bob Dale harvests from the gardens of seven perennial churches principles by which leaders can plant and nurture congregations that thrive rather than simply survive over the years. Dale masterfully tills his newly-found seedbed of organic leadership with living organisms into a readable and practical handbook for 'cultivating perennial churches.' I recommend it to those who are tired of managing organizations and who are ready to get dirt under their fingernails in the garden of people's lives."

C. GENE WILKES, author of *Evangelism Where You Live*

"Bob Dale 'came to church.' Bob got to know us at Second Presbyterian Church and then explained us to ourselves. We felt understood and appreciated. We also were encouraged in our attempts to strive for excellence in ministry. Here's the funny thing about Bob's book, though. Even in reading about the other congregations profiled, my own congregation still was being addressed. In that way, by reading this book, all church leaders will know something of what it is like to have Bob 'come to church.'"

GEORGE C. ANDERSON, Second Presbyterian Church, Roanoke, Virginia

The Columbia Partnership Leadership Series
from Chalice Press

www.chalicepress.com
www.thecolumbiapartnership.org

Cultivating Perennial Churches

Your Guide to Long-Term Growth

ROBERT D. DALE

CHALICE
PRESS

ST. LOUIS, MISSOURI

Scripture quotations, unless otherwise marked, are taken from the HOLY BIBLE, NEW INTERNATIONAL VERSION®. NIV®. Copyright © 1973, 1978, 1984 by International Bible Society. Used by permission of Zondervan Publishing House. All rights reserved.

Cover image: FotoSearch
Cover and interior design: Elizabeth Wright

Visit Chalice Press on the World Wide Web at
www.chalicepress.com

10 9 8 7 6 5 4 3 2 1   08 09 10 11 12

Library of Congress Cataloging–in–Publication Data

Dale, Robert D.
  Cultivating perennial churches : your guide to long-term growth / Robert
D. Dale.
    p. cm.
  ISBN 978-0-8272-0512-3
  1. Church growth—Virginia—Case studies. 2. Church growth—North Carolina—Case studies. I. Title.

BR555.V8D35 2008
254'.5—dc22

                                                          2008023012

Printed in the United States of America

Appreciatively Dedicated to

Carol Barfknecht,
Mary Lou Stephens,
Deannie Butler,
Marilee White,

Co-workers and Co-leaders
across many seasons

Contents

Editor's Foreword

Inspiration and Wisdom for Twenty-First-Century Christian Leaders

You have chosen wisely in deciding to study and learn from a book published in The Columbia Partnership Leadership Series with Chalice Press. We publish for

- Congregational leaders who desire to serve with greater faithfulness, effectiveness, and innovation.
- Christian ministers who seek to pursue and sustain excellence in ministry service.
- Members of congregations who desire to reach their full kingdom potential.
- Christian leaders who desire to use a coach approach in their ministry.
- Denominational and parachurch leaders who want to come alongside affiliated congregations in a servant leadership role.
- Consultants and coaches who desire to increase their learning concerning the congregations and Christian leaders they serve.

The Columbia Partnership Leadership Series is an inspiration- and wisdom-sharing vehicle of The Columbia Partnership, a community of Christian leaders who are seeking to transform the capacity of the North American Protestant church to pursue and sustain vital Christ-centered ministry. You can connect with us at www.TheColumbiaPartnership. org.

Primarily serving congregations, denominations, educational institutions, leadership development programs, and parachurch organizations, the Partnership also seeks to connect with individuals, businesses, and other organizations seeking a Christ-centered spiritual focus.

We welcome your comments on these books, and we welcome your suggestions for new subject areas and authors we ought to consider.

George W. Bullard Jr., Senior Editor
GBullard@TheColumbiaPartnership.org

The Columbia Partnership,
332 Valley Springs Road, Columbia, SC 29223-6934
Voice: 803.622.0923, www.TheColumbiaPartnership.org

Acknowledgments

I've written more than twenty books—mostly based on library research and personal experience. It's not too tough to comment on what others have said and to position your ideas either in agreement or in contrast to them. It's very easy to offer opinions and insights from experience. Those books almost automatically flow out of the word processor in "he said–she said" or "I think" fashion.

But, "growing" a book is an entirely different matter. First, growing anything or anyone is a long-term process. It takes time for people and ideas to mature. When there's almost nothing already written about long-term church growth, you have to go directly to the churches that have grown season after season to see how they've done what they've done. More to the point, when the idea of patiently cultivating church vitality for extended periods of time is not an obvious interest in church growth circles, then you have a doubly difficult task. It isn't easy when you have few resources to draw on and few raving fans to encourage you.

In the beginning, I wasn't sure how to grow a book on perennial church growth, but the process made a mystic of me. Recently, I heard an interview with the British musician Elton John. Commenting on how he wrote his song, "Candle in the Wind," he said, "When in doubt, write a hymn." He then proceeded to play the tune of that song like a hymn being sung in an English cathedral. Without the words, it was a hymn! No wonder it fit the occasion when he sang that song at Princess Diana's funeral. In a way, this book is also a hymn—a praise of God who blesses congregations with health and vigor and a praise of the churches that rely on God rather than gimmicks.

I owe a huge debt of gratitude to the seven pastors—Ronny Russell, Ray Spence, David Bonney, Travis Collins, Gordon Mapes, Bob Disher, and George Anderson—and many other leaders who interpreted these perennial churches to me. These churches' stories deserve to be finally told. I'm also thankful to the people who pointed me toward these seven perennial churches—Rolen Bailey, Donna Hopkins Britt, George Bullard, Franklin Gillis, and Jim Royston. I also appreciate an insightful conversation with Dennis McGuire, founder of Technology Partners Incorporated, a highly successful business services company, on how sustainability can be developed in organizations. I'm indebted to Brian Williams, consistent practitioner of organic leadership, for his inspiration. And, I owe perhaps an even longer-term debt of gratitude to the four administrative assistants—Carol Barfknecht of Nashville,

Tennessee; Mary Lou Stephens of Wake Forest, North Carolina; and Deannie Butler and Marilee White of Richmond, Virginia—to whom this book is dedicated because their workplace partnership helped me grow season after season.

I respect the faith and work of this array of good people and this cluster of perennial churches. Thanks, friends. You've helped me grow over time.

Preface

Learning Longer-term Leadership from Creation

According to the Genesis story of creation, the world was born simply and naturally. God sorted out the original chaos and seeded a burgeoning world. Day by day, the Creator was pleased with the deft touch and the enlivening breath of his craftsmanship. Creation unfolded at God's pace. Everything he touched was good, perfectly good. And, we humans had the best of the best.

We humans enjoyed a garden home. Our first job was to grow things. We were responsible for the garden and for cultivating its living things. The sun and the moon paced the seasons of growth. A tree, the oldest perennial plant on earth, shaded the center of the garden. God was before it all, behind it all, ahead of it all, in it all, and above it all. We happily mirrored our Creator and enjoyed his creation. The future was in motion. It was an elegant paradise.

The garden was a fruitful and productive setting. Swimming things and flying things and walking things flourished. The rains and the winds stimulated God's perfect creation. It was time to change rhythms, to rest from the work of crafting, and to sanctify and celebrate the perfect future.

But, trouble arose in paradise. A reptile, a beast whose ilk is wired always to survive but never to think, tempted the first gardeners to violate the spirit of the garden and the love of the Gardener. That's exactly what we shortsightedly did. By human choice, by our vote, paradise became a broken world. We did it for ourselves and to ourselves. We acted like God had nothing to do with our lives. Then, we left that legacy for humankind's future.

To this day, we're heirs to gardens and trees and reptiles. Like them, we, too, have choices we make day-by-day. Some of our decisions reflect the natural relationships of the original garden. In other choices, we abdicate our futures and leave the world to the instincts of the snake. Fortunately for us, we can still learn from gardens and trees and seasons. Best of all, we can learn from the Gardener and his creative pattern. We can discover ways to relate to living things. We can commit ourselves to the long-term vitality, health, and immunity in our faith communities.

As congregational leaders, we are often pressed to choose shorter term results and set aside longer term harvests. This same dilemma shows up in nature. Some plants are annuals—growing, blooming, and dying in a single season. But perennial plants grow season after season.

In our microwave world, the perennial pattern is too rarely followed by church leaders. This book is intended to challenge shortsightedness and to show the biblical faithfulness of a longer range perennial approach to leadership

What Makes "Perennial Churches" Distinctive and Rare?

What makes the difference? Some congregations are well born and live well. Others are stillborn or get sick and die young. Some barely manage to eke out thin survival. We've seen these patterns. We know the contours of the basic story, don't we? Thankfully, some churches thrive and flourish. But, what makes the difference between congregations showing vitality and the ones that merely hang on?

Church growth literature has typically stressed beginnings. Good start-ups are an understandable growth emphasis. Without a promising birth, churches rarely do well—either short-term or long-range. That's a truism. On the other end of the life cycle, roughly eight of ten American congregations are either static or in decline. We are a bit embarrassed when a congregation actually closes its doors. The implication is that they weren't faithful enough or didn't work hard enough or exercise enough flexibility and creativity.

Maybe there's more to the congregational birth-and-death story than we've told so far. Perhaps there's another dimension to be explored between the "boom beginning" success stories and the "demeaning death" obituaries. What if we seeded and cultivated our congregations for the longer growing season? What if we thought about more than labor pains? What if we led in ways that might grow health and immunity and forestall or avoid death throes?

1

Taking the Longer Look: Perennial Churches in the Spotlight

This book is about church growth and health from a different angle—long-term growth and vitality. From that perspective, we will explore "perennial churches," churches that have grown and stayed vital for 25–30 years or more. These rare churches emphasize:

- More about lasting than starting
- More about God's kingdom than techniques or tricks-of-the-trade
- More about magnetism than magnitude
- More about leading than mimicking

If you're curious about these themes, too, read on. Seven exciting stories of perennial churches will unfold their discoveries.

Life Is a Choice

In a comparative study of societies that collapsed and earned their place in history as failed communities, Jared Diamond[1] notes five broad patterns in cultural ruin and societal death:
Societies die when

- they use up their natural resources or reduce their environment's resiliency to such a marginal level of fragility that the damage is beyond repair. Cutting all of a region's trees and eroding the topsoil, inviting a Dust Bowl that undercuts food production and starves populations is one instance.
- their climates change. Volcanic eruptions, ice ages, and global warming are examples of this threat.
- their neighbors become hostile and attack or at least besiege them. Barbarians at the gates kill cultures as well as populations.
- the neighbors neglect them or withhold support. Friendly neighbors are trading partners and share cultural identities. When friendly interchange wanes, societies are at risk.
- they fail to respond creatively and actively to the challenges arising from the first four issues.

So the basic death sentence of a society may be a lack of imagination and nerve. Death and life are decisions living communities make by their choices and behaviors. For the most part, societies die when they live for the short-term and neglect their future possibilities. They settle to live like annual plants and forget the perennial option of thriving season after season.

Does Diamond have some warning flags for churches? Do congregations also erode themselves to death, fail to adapt to changes, forget to be good neighbors, or, worse yet, do all of the above? What leadership lessons can we learn from the healthiest living communities? How can church leaders leave a long-term legacy rather than simply making a short-term mark in the world? How do churches live or die by their choices and behavior patterns?

Beginning with the Future in Mind

When I read about Japanese bonsai growers handing down their miniature trees from generation to generation as valued parts of their estate, I get a concrete sense of the patience and future-orientation of Eastern culture. That contrasts dramatically with our Western, particularly American, view of production. In the Industrial Age mindset, the productive timeline is extremely short. We usually want more and more, faster and faster, cheaper and cheaper. Sadly, to grow something for our great-grandchildren is beyond our thinking, even as Christians. Isn't that an ironic position for those of us who are invested in eternity?

For the past four hundred years, we Westerners have largely forgotten how to lead living things. Rather, we've thought and acted in mechanical fashion. It's the legacy of the Industrial Era. Communities have been reduced to cogs. Even our congregations and volunteer groups are thought of as machines with compartments and programs and managers. Although the Industrial mindset began to wane in the 1970s, this tenacious viewpoint continues to shape and taint our approach to religious leadership. In contrast, theology has a clear testimony. From a Christian perspective, the church of Jesus Christ is alive. We treat churches as alive and lively, adapting and vital. Christian congregations are alive—it's a basic affirmation of faith.

The Creator God has filled our world with living things—including faith families—as models for learning leadership.[2] The Creator breathed world and Word into existence. That creativity stimulates us to discover ways to be church and to lead churches. Celtic Christians long ago saw the connection between God's world of creation and God's inspired Word. It's an approach we can lean on for our faith, too.

The creation points us toward organic foundations for congregational leaders. Its example offers dynamic guidance to leaders of living communities:

- Believe the church of Jesus Christ is alive.
- Treat congregations as living communities.
- Celebrate that living things change as long as they live.
- Cultivate existing pools of health and energy for growth.
- Invest in roots and immune systems.
- Lead with future seasons in mind.

Are you ready to examine perennial churches and their leaders?

PART I

Planting Perennial Communities

Rooting for the Long Haul

1

Growing Perennially

Our created world enjoys a wide variety of life. In the plant world, we typically distinguish between perennial plants and annuals. It's no surprise that the word *perennial* comes from the Latin term for perpetual. In contrast to annuals with a lifespan of a single growing season, perennials live on and on. They live and grow season after season. That's the simplest answer to what makes perennials—plants or churches—special. But, that's only part of the story. Not only do perennials survive, they also can and do thrive.

Perennials—royalty in the world of living and growing things—have the knack of living on and on. This book profiles a cluster of perennial churches, those special and unusual congregations with long growth arcs and extended lifetimes of vigor. While these churches typify a specific aspect of perennial life, they also embody the larger cluster of characteristics of perennials. They help raise and answer a key question: what helps churches thrive, adapt, and grow over a quarter century or more?

Cut Flowers versus Perennial Growth

We Westerners live in a "cut flower" world, according to some observers. We Americans are an especially impatient people. We demand instant gratification, quick fixes, fast food, short cuts, winning streaks, and overnight success. We want our church growth microwave fast and dramatic as well. We Americans expect our religion to provide quick payoffs, like annual plants that flower rapidly in a single growing season.

Consequently, we're too willing to cut our religious flowers early and to start over every season. In the same vein, our church growth stories concentrate on big beginnings, boom churches, and impressive short-term attendance numbers.

Although he was describing American values when he lamented our "cut flower" civilization, Elton Trueblood[1] depicted our impatient Western churches as well. Cut flowers may be showy, dramatic, and beautiful, but they have no root system and, therefore, no future. Trueblood called for reinvigorated faith to provide roots and durability for our world. He wanted religious faith in the West to have the strength to sustain ethical, moral, and social leadership perennially in our culture.

Trueblood saw clearly that faith is a journey, not a jiffy. That's true for both personal faith and congregational life. Healthy growth takes time. Christian faith is a lifestyle rather than a magic formula. The old English adage for how perennials grow may be true for many living communities:

"First year sleeps,
second year creeps,
third year leaps."

While strategic patience is required in all healthy churches, some congregations are "perennials"—successful and durable, rooted and identified, flourishing and reproducing year after year.

Profiling Perennial Churches

For purposes of this study, the seven churches profiled here share three broad-based, defining marks of ministry.

1. Perennial churches have healthy 25–30 year or longer growth arcs, showing durability, vitality, and creativity.
2. Perennial churches grow, adapt, and multiply their ministries steadily. They are both productive and reproductive.
3. Perennial churches live and thrive over time, cultivating their core identity without fads and in less than perfect conditions.

What explains their growth and steadfastness? Why do some congregations deepen, heighten, and widen their reach and outreach over time? Which characteristics of perennial plants do these congregations demonstrate year after year? Their stories will be told by their sources, but the leadership interpretation emerging from those stories will be mine alone.

Seven Strengths: A Perennial Primer

Botanically, a perennial—literally "through" plus "year"—is a plant that produces flowers and seeds through more than one year. Perennials give us lots to eat and enjoy. Fruit and nut trees provide significant amounts of food for humans. Shrubs and flowers provide color and texture in yards and habitats. And, turf grasses for lawns are now the biggest agricultural cash crop in America.[2] Perennials are important to us. In simplest botanical terms, perennials live on season after season.

Specifically, other than mere length of life, perennials contrast with annual plants in at least seven significant ways. Does the same cluster of seven strengths apply to congregations, too? What can congregational leaders discover about planting for health and immunity season after season?

#1–Perennials Reflect Their Planters' Purpose

The seeds or root stocks of annuals and perennials look pretty much alike to the naked eye. The blooms are similar. But their life spans and growth arcs are dramatically different. The difference in most annual and perennial gardens is in the design. Perennials are usually planted with more deliberation since they'll be back again in a new season. Garden design is shaped by what their gardeners intend when they place perennials in the soil at planting time. Some gardeners are freestyle, creating the look of a wildflower meadow. Other gardeners are precise, crafting English gardens with their carefully shaped and manicured contours. It depends on the gardener's intention and purpose.

Congregations are called to serve as cultivators of God's kingdom. Soul gardening[3] is the sole redemptive purpose of congregations and believers. There's no other reason for Christian ministry—nothing more, nothing less, nothing else—than planting and nurturing the reign of God in individual lives and in human history. We are Christian disciples who reproduce Christian disciples (Mt. 28:19–20).

The kingdom of God is the spotlighted theological theme in the New Testament. Not only was the kingdom of God the theme Jesus taught and preached primarily during his ministry, the same emphasis also continues throughout the New Testament. For example, the book of Acts is the chronicle of the early church's expansion. That book begins and ends with its message rooted firmly in the kingdom of God. In the opening paragraph of the book (Acts 1:3), Jesus spoke of the kingdom of God after his resurrection. In the final verse of the book, Paul preached the kingdom of God in his waning days (Acts 28:31). Like bookends, God's kingdom brackets not only the book of Acts, but all we do as Christian disciples and witnesses.

Coaching Questions to Help Your Church Look at Its Original Purposes

- How does our church cultivate Christian disciples for the "kingdom of God"?

- Have we practiced these core Christian beliefs from our beginnings?
- What seeds or root stock were planted here originally?
- How has the DNA of our congregation consistently maintained itself over time?
- What's the most distinctive, long-term ministry of our congregation?
- What's our congregation's "claim to fame"?
- How is the kingdom of God reflected in our ministry pattern?

#2–Perennials Grow Stronger Root Systems

Perennials gather water and nutrients more efficiently, thereby getting a running start when new growing seasons emerge. Prairie grasses, 99 percent of which are perennials, are vivid examples of perennials' sturdy root networks. Jon Piper, expert on the diversity of prairie grasses, points out that 70 percent of the living weight of prairies is underground. Like an underground neighborhood, the prairie's root systems are made up of "the nitrogen fixers, the deep-rooted ones that dig for water, the shallow-rooted ones that make the most of a gentle rain, the ones that grow quickly in the spring to shade out weeds, the ones that resist pests or harbor heroes such as beneficial insects."[4] The majority of the prairie grass is unseen, a sturdy system of roots. But, without roots, there are no shoots.

Look at the shade trees in your yard. Most of them have root systems that extend out three times beyond the diameter of the leafy canopy. They sink roots deep and wide before they contribute shade, fruit, nuts, and flowers to their environs. It's no accident that trees are the longest-living organisms on earth. They have great root systems.

How can we know we're being true to a faith community's root system? In the so-called social sector, the Cleveland Orchestra is an interesting case study.[5] Tom Morris became the executive director in 1987 with a simple mandate—make a great orchestra even greater. But, how do you know an orchestra is growing from great to greater and improving in the eyes of the community? Morris helped the orchestra examine its performance to be sure it was superior, its impact to be sure it was distinctive, and its contribution to be sure it was enduring.

"Superior performance" by the orchestra was observed in several strategic responses:

- more standing ovations by audiences
- a wider range of difficult musical selections in performances
- an increasing demand for tickets
- more invitations for repeat concert performances in America and Europe

"Distinctive impact" was seen in a variety of patterns

- programming styles copied by others
- increasing civic pride as noticed in Clevelanders bragging about the orchestra
- providing a setting for grief with a concert two nights after 9–11
- leavening the community through the leadership of orchestra members

"Lasting endurance" was confirmed by an array of "heritage" behaviors:

- sustaining musical excellence across generations of conductors
- broadening and deepening the donor and endowment bases
- strengthening the orchestra's organization during and after Tom Morris' tenure

Roots and foundations are critical to long-term stability and productivity. The orchestra flourished by drawing on its deep root system.

Coaching Questions to Guide Your Church in Exploring Its Root System

- How has our church rooted itself in ways that have created foundations for longer-term growth?
- How has our church been faithful to its root system and longer-term values? How have we clarified our identity in Christ?
- How have we taken time to build good foundations here?
- How do we anticipate what comes next and change from our root system?

#3–Perennials Are Resilient and Tough

Perennials don't require ideal, hospitable, or resource-rich conditions to flourish. Perennials cover and hold soil better than annuals. They may even enrich their seedbeds themselves; 30% of the root systems of prairie grasses are self-fertilizing, decaying into the soil to add organic matter.[6] They "invest" in the stewardship of their setting. Legumes, plants that store up necessary nitrogen in their root systems, combine crop yield with enrichment for their own seedbeds.[7] Additionally, perennials show resilience. They resist "plagues" better—coping with pests,[8] resisting disease, and weathering drought well.

Annual plants tend to be selfish. Most annuals are purchased in garden shops already in bloom. They're at or near their peaks when they go in the ground. Annuals have a one-season life span and compete to get everything they can while they can. They put nothing back into their seedbeds. They have no sense of stewardship.

Churches may adopt an annual mindset, too. They may see every other church or helping agency as a rival. They want a clear field all to themselves, making their own survival paramount. When they feel crowded or threatened, they may fight off their rivals, move to greener pastures, or simply wall themselves off and function in isolation.

Coaching Questions about Your Church's Sturdiness and Durability

- What has been the most traumatic situation our church has faced, a decision or detour that could have derailed it?
- When have we been closest to death?
- How have we stayed steady and faithful when circumstances pressured us to choose lesser options?
- Have we grown beyond community conditions here?
- What has happened in neighboring churches over the past 20–25 years?
- Has our vitality been more theologically based or sociologically based?
- Are we strong because of what we believe and practice, or do we depend on favorable neighborhood demographics and expansion?
- What challenges have appeared here over and over again? How have they been faced?
- Have we seen our ministry context enriched? Have we "built up our seedbeds"?

#4–Perennials Thrive in "Mixed Meadows"

Perennials usually grow amid blends of plants. The tall grass prairies of the American West typically mixed four types of grasses and other plants. The prairies were examples of one truth in the perennial world: the best hedge against disaster is variety.[9] However, in the nearly 10,000 years since the advent of agriculture, we have steadily chosen to base our food supply on annual crops. That decision has discounted perennials as important sources of nourishment. We've migrated toward the quick (and the quickly dead) in our food supply.

During the first two centuries of American history, new church starts were generally intentional attempts to reach entire and intact neighborhoods. Then, late in the twentieth century, the homogenous growth principle began to be applied in church growth. New starts were designed to become communities of like minds and compatible lifestyles by helping "birds of a feather flock together." Although sometimes regional in outreach, these congregations were largely populated by members who were alike in background, income, education, and outlook. "Mixed meadows" were ignored.

The Pentecost story in Acts 2 shows that the Gospel appeals to all people, and the Holy Spirit reaps in diverse fields. Think of it. The gathered crowd heard the preachers in their own languages—Parthians, Medes, Elamites, Mesopotamians, Judeans, Cappadocians, natives of Pontus, Asians, Phrygians, Egyptians, Libyans, Romans, Cretans, and Arabs (Acts 2:5–12). The Christian movement was planted and thrived in mixed meadows.

Coaching Questions to Consider about Ministry amid Diversity

- How have we diversified and added new ministries while keeping core ministries healthy?
- Have we bridged cultures and ministries here for growth?
- How have we dealt with diverse challenges?
- How has consistent direction been preserved amid multiple challenges here?
- How have we dealt with ministry fads?

#5–Perennials Grow from a Variety of Beginnings

Most annuals are grown from seeds or by transplanting small plants. Growing from seeds, roots, cuttings, and division, perennials' beginnings spring from a variety of sources. Perennials exercise more flexibility than annuals in their beginnings. Seeds, bulbs, and divisions of older plants are common launch points for perennials. Dividing mature plants every three-to-five years allows old plants to get a new lease on life, controls the size of existing plants, and multiplies the numbers of perennials in the garden. Flexibility aids survival and opens the door for longer-term thriving.

Some church growth specialists have "the method" for starting new churches. I recently saw one successful church planter lose his temper during a seminar because questions were asked about his approach. The questioner was seeking understanding, but the expert felt his style was being devalued. He was angered by the implication that other approaches might also work. I guess he wasn't thinking of mixed meadows.

Coaching Questions to Clarify the Range of Factors in Your Church's Launch

- How has our church benefited from being planted from multiple sources?
- How many different approaches have we used to plant new ministries here over time?
- How have we kept current growth from crowding future growth?
- Have we grown mostly by extension and division or by expansion of new ministries?

#6–Perennials Grow during All Seasons

Perennials are "three season" growers. They produce during spring, summer, and fall. Then, like most plants and some animals, perennials go into dormancy in cold weather climates during the winter season. But, their root systems remain alive and well, giving them a running start on new growing seasons. The obvious point here is that freezing doesn't kill off perennials. Their hardiness and their deep root systems insulate and sustain them in the face of challenging circumstances.

Gardeners appreciate the cyclical nature of perennials. These growers always have beauty emerging in their flowerbeds as well as beauty to anticipate in later cycles of growth. Using a three-season bloom strategy, they plan for living pictures outdoors during spring, summer, and fall. Churches pace themselves for three reasons: they give the Spirit time to work, they harvest only when the yield is ripe, and they take time to pace themselves and avoid burnout.

"All Seasons" Coaching Questions for Your Church

- Have we cultivated the rhythms of congregational life? Are we "three season" growers?
- How have we paced ministries here across time?
- How well do we cultivate cycles of intensity with times of respite, periods of racing with periods of pacing? When do we plant, and when do we let the ground rest and lay fallow?
- When does our congregation show the most energy? When is it most at rest?
- What core ministries never go dormant around here?
- How have we "harvested" ministries that were past their prime and then moved ahead?

#7–Perennials Reproduce with the Future in Mind

Here in my home region of central Virginia, lawns are planted or overseeded in the fall. It's called "the SOD method" for September and October through December. Plant in September, then water and protect from October to December—that's the approach. The reason is simple. Fescue and other turf grasses, if planted in the cool weather months, will sink their roots into the soil quickly and withstand the cold of winter. Then, when the spring's warmth arrives, these grasses are poised to get a head start on other plants. The horticulturists remind us—first roots, then shoots. This principle applies to churches even more than lawns.

Christianity is faith with a long history and a vigorous hope. Specific events in the faith story occurred at identifiable points in time. We remember and celebrate Abraham, Isaac, and Jacob; Saul, David, and Solomon; Isaiah, Jeremiah, and Amos; Jesus, Paul, and the heroes of more contemporary ministry. We stand within a faith tradition. We have a story to tell again and again. We are guided by a liturgical year. In other words, Christianity understands seasonality. We also practice hope. We believe God holds history in His hands. He commands futures.

Coaching Questions about Present Status and Future Possibilities for Your Church

- How have we grown a promising future from a sturdy past?
- Can we seize God's best futures, while still staying true to our roots?
- How can we evaluate our church's ministries intentionally and seasonally?
- What are our church's futures?

Perennial Profiles

The seven congregations profiled in the case histories that follow reflect the seven unique characteristics of perennial plants. Honestly, each of these churches show most or all of the distinctive qualities of perennials. But each characteristic is matched with *one* church as a leadership case study in growth and health over time.

These congregational profiles are stories. That's appropriate because stories of faith, testimonies of God-at-work in life, are a way we witness to the life of God in our lives. Personal stories of faith are part personal biography and part mystic memoirs. These personal faith narratives become more complex when they become community stories, when they are multiplied by the number of members in the entire congregation. Faith stories speak of both salvation and of sin, because we humans are flawed. We're a bit like a Navajo rug. When Navajo rug makers weave a rug, they deliberately put a flaw in it. Their reasoning is simple: only God is perfect. These seven churches aren't perfect, but they've shown their faithfulness to God season after season.

Leadership case studies are a common strategy for understanding how communities behave. The method is straightforward:

- A single issue is spotlighted. In this instance, the focal concern is why and how congregations have sustained growth and vitality across a minimum sweep of 25–30 years or longer.
- The living historical context is explored in depth. On-site interviews with current leaders and research of documents and records provide firsthand information and longer-term perspective on the lives of these perennial congregations. The questions from earlier in this chapter help frame the face-to-face conversations with leaders.

Illustrations, vignettes, and stories, rather than formal or technical histories, are used to describe the settings and circumstances in which decisions were made, actions taken, and ministry solutions uncovered. In other words, congregational leadership is the focus you'll encounter again and again in this book.

As a consequence of using a leadership case history approach, you'll read and compare the following:

- Profiles of congregational ministry and leadership
- Leadership applications of perennials' characteristics
- Patterns of leadership
- Implications for congregational leaders

We should remind ourselves that the leaders of the seven profiled churches were simply trying to serve the kingdom of God. They weren't deliberately intending to teach us how to lead in ways that grow perennial churches. But, we have the advantage of time and an outsider's perspective. We can look over their shoulders and learn. We can see what they did and what we can do. Hopefully, from this angle, we can see the bigger picture and sense broader implications. Learning from the distances of time and perspective provides us some leadership rehearsal. We can "open off-Broadway" before we're faced with all the demands of congregational leadership.

Mapping the Perennial Garden

Seven cases, a limited sample, are presented here. Even though seven is considered a perfect number in biblical studies, it's a minimum landscape for leaders. Only churches from Reformation traditions are profiled here, and only the Mid-Atlantic region of the United States is considered. You're invited to test the principles of perennial leadership, to expand the experience and research base geographically and denominationally, and to enhance your own ability to help God grow our congregations season after season. It's worth reminding ourselves that perennial plants—and perennial churches—have no lifetime guarantees. Studies of great companies remind us that it's the rarest of organizations that grows forever. But, some faith communities thrive over long periods of time, or, as described here, they grow perennially.

Listed below are the seven perennial churches chosen for our study, along with the perennial characteristics that are featured in their cases. The theme running throughout all of our cases is how to lead these rare congregations that are in Kingdom ministry for the long haul. You'll read about old churches that become young again, churches that nearly die and then rise from the dead, churches that creatively interact with their communities and world, and churches that produce change in their ministry settings and beyond. These churches range from nearly two hundred years old to only thirty years of ministry. Here's the lineup.

Mission Baptist Church in Locust, N.C., reflects the design of a purposive perennial congregation. This church is more than one hundred years old and has been transformed into a focused, consistent disciple-making community of faith in recent years.

Second Baptist Church in Richmond, Va., is an example of a rooted perennial congregation. Second's beginning DNA is reflected throughout its nearly two-hundred-year ministry. Season after season, through good times and bad, Second Baptist has lived and ministered out of its deep and strong root system.

Saint Mark's United Methodist Church, Midlothian, Va., exemplifies a resilient perennial congregation. Unlike many congregations that are spotlighted in some church growth studies, Saint Mark's has been challenged with difficulties along its path and looked death in the eye, but it has responded with new vitality and steadiness.

Bon Air Baptist Church in Richmond, Va., is an example of a diverse perennial congregation. Bon Air has cultivated a "mixed meadow" of missions and ministries and has developed an array of outreaches to its community and world.

The *Brandermill Church, Midlothian, Va.,* an ecumenical congregation with Presbyterian and Methodist ties, lives out the advantages of a flexible perennial congregation. For thirty years, this unique church has shown internal strength and external sensitivity.

St. Mark's Reformed Church, Burlington, N.C., began as a German-speaking congregation for immigrant farmers in North Carolina's Piedmont region in the mid-1800s. It's now a regional church in multiple sites and a model of a productive perennial congregation.

Second Presbyterian Church, Roanoke, Va., a historic, century-old church with a bright future, is a clear example of a futuristic perennial congregation. This congregation has built on its identity to claim its tomorrows and is moving forward deliberately and faithfully.

The Seed Catalog

Now it's time to look at the profiles of these seven perennial congregations and their leadership patterns. Enjoy the lessons of churches that have grown God-ward season after season.

2

Leading Purposive Perennials

Mission Baptist Church, Locust, N.C.

Building the Hub from the Rim

Mission Baptist Church lives on the edge of "the Hub,"[1] the metropolitan region sprawling out from Charlotte, North Carolina. Since the edges or margins of cultures are always the liveliest, Mission is now sharing the dynamic growth of the Hub and is depending increasingly on its much larger neighbor to the west for information, income, transportation, and services. The Hub lies astride the border of two states, at the intersection of two interstate highways, I-85 and I-77, serves as an airline hub for U.S. Airways, has become the sixth largest distributor of goods in the United States, and hosts national and international headquarters of major financial institutions, including Bank of America and First Union Bank.

In many ways, Charlotte is a MBA town, a city of self-starters and ladder climbers. They might pursue upward mobility even faster except for the gridlock on the roads and streets. Charlotte's traffic makes it a "hurry up and wait" city. One soccer mom, stuck in her minivan in a long line of traffic at an intersection while running a routine errand, showed desperation. She pressed a hand-lettered sign against her vehicle's windshield: "I just want some milk!"

In contrast, Mission, in western Stanly County[2], is only forty minutes but nearly a lifetime away from the congestion and press of downtown Charlotte. Buffered from the Hub geographically by the fringes of other counties, Mission's members enjoy a slower, more rural, and more blue collar lifestyle. If Charlotte is "the bank," or the financial center of the larger region, Mission's members are the small business operators and construction workers who are building that bank.

Mission's members may depend on the Hub for many things, but they choose a freer atmosphere for home and faith out on the rim of the Hub. The outlying area around the town of Locust, the little city of a few more than 2500 citizens near Mission, is growing. It's home to young families, becoming more affluent, pleased to enjoy a less hectic pace of life, and proud of their community and schools. West Stanly High School boasts about its' students' SAT scores and claims "WEST" stands for "Where Excellence Starts Today."

Slow and Steady

Mission has a long history in ministry. In 1880, E.P. Harrington, a Baptist preacher who had been invited to visit a prayer meeting in the area, found a liquor store and gambling establishment near the site of the present church and described the field as "a place that needs Christian work."[3] Mission was formally organized in 1883 as Elizabeth Baptist Church, taking its current name in 1895. Its early days were hardscrabble, including meeting in a brush arbor until 1910. The primary church building was dedicated in 1924. Momentum built after World War II with some membership growth and completion of a series of facility expansions—an educational building in 1956, a fellowship building in 1962, a new worship center in 1970, and a recreation area with a lighted tennis court in 1975. Former high school teacher and fledgling pastor, Ronny Russell, arrived in 1974, fresh from seminary, twenty-seven years old, ready to serve energetically and to learn his pastoral craft.

Like many novice pastors, Ronny set out to do what he knew to do—preach, visit, and make friends. Soon, he was the "village priest,"[4] pastor to virtually everyone in the community. The church grew slowly but steadily. By 1976, Mission's membership totaled 265. In true perennial fashion, Mission was following the "sleep, creep, leap" pattern described in the model chapter. Progress was slow and steady for the church.

Treadmills Don't Move Ahead

But Mission's pastor was also slowly and steadily burning out. People in the giving professions are always at risk of hitting the spiritual and emotional wall of depletion. A therapist in a former church described to me the toll a full day of counseling took on him. He said the final counselees for each day always seemed to arrive with their umbilical cords in their hands, looking hungrily to plug themselves into a new source of life. He noted that being everything to everybody sometimes means they take everything from you. The neediest personalities, he said, invite you to pedal along on eternal treadmills to nowhere.

Ronny, the "holy handyman,"[5] understood the toll of that treadmill. As his workload expanded, his mood became more depressed; and his cynicism grew. Finally, in 1993, he had a heart attack. Like Moses, he was living on the back side of the desert at midlife and was ripe for a new sense of direction in ministry. It was time to get off the treadmill. It was time for a transition, a new direction, for Ronny and for Mission. But, what direction should be chosen? He addressed the congregation and challenged the members to seize a new future. Two responses emerged. Some said, "Let's try something." Another group of generally younger members said, "You've described what we're supposed to do. Let's go."

Ronnie and Mission grew together and moved forward deliberately. The story of how Mission became a purposive perennial church will feature Ronny's role prominently. The reason is straightforward: gardeners design their flowerbeds. Purposive leaders don't set the direction alone, but their part is crucial.

One Tree—The Key to a Straight Row

When leaders determine they're not in the right place in their ministry, they are faced with making some choices and selecting a direction for themselves. At this point, most ministers move to a new field and get on a new treadmill. But, for those who stay in the familiar place, the task is tougher. Discerning new directions isn't easy, automatic, or obvious. To confound the process even more, the leader faces lots of competing options to consider.

Direction demands a deliberate decision. I grew up on a river bottom farm in Southwest Missouri where we grew livestock and grain. Corn was our key cash grain crop. So, I learned to plant, cultivate, and harvest corn before I was a teenager. Farmers in our part of the world grew a strange pride about planting straight rows of corn. They found artistry to it. Somehow, the symmetry of the field was virtually sacred to us and our neighbors. People bragged about the elegant craftsmanship revealed by a straight row. Or, perversely, they gossiped about how sloppy and unkempt a crooked corn row looked from the road!

That mythical straight row wasn't easy to create. Our own cornfields, carved out by the river, were irregularly shaped. With the river on one side, a bluff on a second side, and mountains on a third side, a planter had no straight fence rows and nothing to guide toward a true row. So, my Dad taught me a simple procedure for planting a straight row.

Go to the center. Estimating the center point of the field, position the corn planter there. Choose a target. Select a tree in the center at the opposite end of the field as your point of reference. Don't take your eyes off the target. There must be no wandering and absolutely no deviations. Steer unerringly to that target. Drive carefully, firmly, and relentlessly toward that single tree.

The entire field, then, is oriented by that first row. We called this procedure "laying off the field." The straightness of that initial row determined whether our neighbors were proud of us that particular growing season, or whether they just gossiped behind our backs about how we'd wandered off course and had sown a cornfield that shamed the entire community!

Design for the Future

The search for an orientation point, a foundational purpose, is the journey Ronny began in the early 1990s. He deepened his self-understanding by doing a unit of clinical pastoral education. He read books on church renewal. He attended conferences on congregational revitalization. How could he and the other church leaders choose one seed to plant in the center of Mission's garden? Finally, the focus became clear in the last will and testament of a person Ronny had known for a long time. He had read the words often before, but now, placed at the center of Mission's ministry, the familiar phrases drew him like a magnet: "Go and make disciples of all nations, baptizing them in the name of the Father and of the Son and of the Holy Spirit, and teaching them to obey everything I have commanded you" (Mt. 28:19–20a). Ronny realized the first calling of a congregation is disciple-making. He had found the landmark toward which he'd steer his ministry. Then, the question was how to drive steadily toward that landmark.

Ministers are rarely trained for purposeful invention. We have been more schooled in the care of others than the care of our own selves and souls, more instructed in the "old, old story" than the new, new world. Many of us are products of denominations with "programs," a prepackaged one-size-fits-all ministry model. We're generally imitators. In a stable situation in a steady world, programs were pretty effective. But, ministry demands have changed more than we have in recent years. We're still ill-equipped to deal with the challenges of designing new ministries. Maybe every minister needs to become a master gardener. Then, we'd be better equipped to work with the "now" and the "not yet" of living things, especially faith communities.

Designing the future of a living faith community is a bit like the process a perennial gardener follows in laying out and tending a new flowerbed. In broad terms, here's what gardeners do to create a beautiful landscape.[6] It's easy to see that congregational leaders use similar approaches to grow their leader corps and their communities of faith.

- Refine your ideas and options. Do research.[7] Read. Ask questions of folks who have done this before. Go to workshops. Get a coach. Visit other successful sites. From all your observation and effort, identify an array of options that could match the uniqueness of your field of ministry.
- Be site-specific. What grows in one place may not fit another setting. Know where the sun and water and wind—the power sources and the hindrances—move across your site.
- Understand your own strengths, preferences, and gifts. Do what you do best. Go with your gifts. Grow what you enjoy most. Ask, "What energizes me?"
- Sketch a plan. Plan for a panorama of colors and textures. Then, experiment. Be ready to "muddle" while change sorts itself out. Set a direction, but be ready and willing to adjust as needed. Most perennial gardeners are willing to move a slow-growing or struggling plant to a more compatible spot in the flowerbed at least once or twice.
- Create a focal point. Spotlight one special planting. Let it draw the eye. Make it the center of what's routinely seen and displayed.
- Take the time and invest the effort to place the best seeds in the best soil. Plant well, feed well, and water well. Taking extra care in planting and cultivating will bring better yields at harvest time.
- Place compatible perennials together. Let them complement each other. Remember that perennials like the company of other plants and thrive in mixed meadows.
- Follow the rhythms of growth. Some plants develop early, and others later. Know the patterns of your perennials. Let the overall plan unfold over time, over seasons, over years. Sailors will tell you it takes time and fifty miles of ocean to turn and redirect a big ship.

A good design is apt to grow a good future. Notice how what a master gardener does to design a perennial garden can be applied to congregational direction or redirection? With a central belief for ministry practice, Ronny set out to grow himself and to grow others.

One Root System: A Theology of Principle

Finding bedrock to build on, Ronny began clarifying and applying a few basic principles he would use in making disciples—he would spotlight the Great Commission, he would invest in his own growth and in the development of a leader corps first, and he would then challenge those disciples to reach out and change the world.

Disciple-making, a Biblical Baseline

Ronny found one like-minded resource group in T-Net International in Aurora, Colorado.[8] T-Net sees itself as a ministry that's completing the Great Commission by helping churches intentionally disciple Christian believers. This coaching organization calls itself the Training Network for Disciplemaking Churches. It grew from a pastor's commitment to return his church to its disciple-making roots.

Using older Industrial Age images, T-Net contrasts "warehouse churches" and "factory churches." Warehouses stockpile and preserve material, while factories take raw materials, transform them, and send the new products out into the marketplace. T-Net intends to create more "factory churches." To describe the goal more biblically and organically, churches such as Mission are cultivating believers and growing them into disciples of Christ. The process of soul gardening[9] brings people to faith, roots them in basic faith and practices, helps them discover and pursue their ministries, and trains them to grow other disciples.

T-Net uses a four-phase discipleship process:

1. "Come and See"—This phase attracts and evangelizes people into a relationship with Christ, hopefully in a short time period.
2. "Come and Follow Me"—This phase roots new believers in basic Christian patterns of believing and behaving, taking a year or less.
3. "Come and Be with Me"—This phase trains and deploys Christian disciples as ministers and leaders, lasting a couple of years.
4. "Remain in Me"—This lifelong phase aims at multiplying disciple-makers.

Ronny began using T-Net in 1994, along with a variety of other approaches, to call Mission's members to faith and discipleship. The theological baseline remained the Great Commission, the call to make disciples. What has Ronny learned from a decade of disciple-making? In part, Mission has become less "religious" and more redemptive, less managerial and more "missional."[10]

Growing Leaders First, Grow Change Later

Ronny concentrated on planting the seeds to grow disciples into maturity and into leadership. Beyond the disciplines of study, prayer, and ministry, three types of relationships were deliberately developed.

1. Unity through regular worship.
2. Fellowship through the Sunday school classes of Mission.
3. Intimacy through a new cluster of small groups.

The distinctive element in this process was that leaders were grown first, in advance of major responsibilities. The larger membership of Mission would follow in the disciple-making process later. Accountability was expected of Mission's members, including giving and cultivating others toward faith in Christ.

Reaching out as Christ's Disciples

Ronny pointed out that Christ's disciples aren't satisfied to study and pray in privacy or isolation. Disciples are called to move out, leaven their personal spheres of influence, and, ultimately, change their worlds. They reach out in missions and evangelism. Mission began living out its name in practical expressions of Christian love. In the spirit of servant evangelism, Mission did simple things. For example, they staffed concession stands at school events so parents could be more involved with their children. Mission used the "hands-on" model of connecting to its community through "Operation Inasmuch."[11]

In 1999, Mission responded to the needs of Hurricane Mitch's victims in Honduras, rebuilding homes and churches. That initial trip began a creative new pattern. The church has returned to the same village in Honduras more than ten times so far, the same general location in Mexico three times, and the same overall Katrina recovery regional site four times. Mission's patient pattern of disciple-making has yielded relational depth and long-term ties. Outreach projects first become places of ministry and then they become faces and friendships. Mission has used an adopt-a-kid approach in Honduras to provide scholarships for more than one hundred children of the village. Mission's team members are learning Spanish to communicate more personally during future Honduran visits.

Feeding the Roots: Pinches Germinate Change

Leaders of perennial churches use challenge to face challenges. They know that complacent persons don't grow readily. They expect resistance.

Stretching with Challenge

Disciple-making at Mission uses multiple resources for challenge—sermons, columns in newsletters, Web messages, "bubble up" people, and "outside prophets." Faith communities need "stretch" to grow and mature. "Bubble up" people are a community's innovators who are willing to press against the status quo. They stir the pot and create ferment. "Outside prophets" challenge the community as well. Eddie Hammett, a congregational coach, has been involved with Mission as a conference leader and prophetic voice for nearly a decade. After one pivotal retreat session in which Eddie persisted in exploring why a member had had trouble fitting into the congregation's life, Ronny reported, "Only an outside prophet could have done what he did that night—and lived to tell about it!"[12] Challenge is necessary for growth.

Spreading Viral Vision

A common vision is contagious and sprouts from multiple roots. Mission has budgeted to send lay leaders to training conferences. Ronny has encouraged leaders to read contemporary Christian thinkers or "prophets in paperback" and to go on mission trips. He sees and uses the viral impact of Jesus' model of inviting the Twelve to be with him and to learn from him directly.

Expecting the Act-React Cycle

Change is constant in living things, but it never becomes comfortable. We always are tempted to go back to the way we were. To move forward, faith communities need expansion joints, like bridges. These spreading panels can absorb and cushion some of the strain of change.

At one juncture in Mission's move toward disciple-making, a room change was needed. Ronny went to talk to the group who used the room for Sunday school. They'd been in that space a long time. They'd paid for the curtains and carpet in the space. When Ronny told them the church needed their space for other purposes, the group resisted. In fact, they became known among church leaders as the "We Shall Not Be Moved" class. After a few weeks, they agreed to move for the sake of congregational growth. But, they illustrated the predictable action-gets-a-reaction cycle. Resisting change is a natural reaction, not a matter of good or bad people or good or bad changes.

Following the Seasons: Patience and Pacing

In some long distance races, one runner is assigned the "rabbit" responsibility. That runner sets the pace for those who will go the distance. The rabbit sets the stage for good times. When the rabbit steps off the track at about mid-race, the rest of the race depends on conditioning and strategy.

Building on the Reservoir of Trust and Relationships

Twenty years of home and hospital visits, marrying and burying, praying and preaching creates lots of trusting relationships. As Ronny describes it, faithful ministry across many years earns "an entry into the lives of people."[13] Listening to others makes them more apt to listen to you. Durable connections to the community cultivate trust in leaders for the future.

Thinking Seasons, Not Seconds

It takes time for the roots of change to flower. Not all leaders are willing to cultivate and wait. Since trust is fragile, slow to build, and quick to break, leaders need a sense of timing about how change unfolds.

Ronny had a call from a Texas pastor about turnaround dynamics. The Texan was an ex-Marine who had a "see a hill, take a hill" mentality. That quick-fix approach had spurred several episodes of conflict in his church. Perennials take seasons, not seconds, to grow. Leaders cultivate horizons.

Preparing Hearts with Prayer

Prayer undergirds Mission's ministries. For instance, the Honduras trips are preceded with overnight retreats for prayer, reading, and fasting and followed up with debriefing and reports to the congregation. Disciple-making never stops. Neither does the prayer.

Not All Plants Live: The Price of Cultural Change

Nothing much changes without pain. Don't expect communities to adjust the way they do things or change their make-up without some discomfort. There's always a price in growing. Don't underestimate the disappointments or harden your heart against the human costs of change.

Slip-sliding Away, Feeling the Pain of Loss

Even stable churches occasionally lose members. Congregations that grow and change typically lose members, too. Ronny reports some losses at Mission. "It is difficult…to watch people walk away. Usually these are people in whom a pastor and others have invested time and energy. Ministers may have celebrated with those people the birth of children or grandchildren, mourned the death of loved ones, played golf, eaten dinner, and counted them among their best friends. This has happened more than once at Mission, and let me tell you it hurts every time."[14]

I've seen this phenomenon of loss in many dynamic churches. The difference I see in Ronny is pastoral pain at the forty or fewer members who left over ten years. There's no resigning himself to exits, and, better yet, no joy in these departures. Some pastors seem to go out of their ways to divide the house, create factions, write off "the other side" as enemies, and take some satisfaction in the loss of certain members. I heard one pastor claim he had to run off seven hundred members to save his church. I'd have preferred to see a pastoral heart broken by the debris of exits.

Energy Toll on Leaders

Moving a congregation from maintenance ministry to missional ministry is taxing. It drains emotional and spiritual resources. Is it worth it? Ronny admits that the toll of missional ministry is constant and eroding. He says, "I don't believe I would have the energy to do it again in another church. It is a lifetime endeavor."[15] That admission tells us why so few perennial churches exist. Leaders are called on to commit, work, stay, and give everything to the making of disciples.

Profiling Purposive Perennial Leaders

Leaders of purposive perennial congregations patiently grow themselves and others for the future. How does an "outside prophet"[16] see Ronny's strengths as a purposive perennial leader?

- He's a risk taker (who) moves through his dissatisfaction to find dreams.
- He's an equipper and one who doesn't do ministry in selfish ways.
- He shares the blessing with others.
- He enjoys diversity and new things.
- He's a lifelong learner.
- He really believes and practices good discipleship.

Leading Purposive Perennials

It's tempting to think of Mission as a turnaround story. And, it is. But, the real story, the story behind the turnaround, is how it became a purposive perennial church. After nearly a century of life and ministry, how did Mission become more purposive? More to the point, how are purposive perennial congregations best lead?

Purposive Leaders Take a Steady, Long View

Purposive leaders understand the typical perennial cycle of "sleep, creep, and leap." They patiently realize living communities move at their own built-in paces. They realistically recognize that surprises and second-order effects are to be expected—but usually aren't. They are on the lookout for watershed years, when tipping points occur and life is different from that juncture forward. They not only think about what comes next—they also wonder about what will come after what comes next. They know transformational growth in persons and communities takes seasons, decades, and even God's eternity.

When you've served as pastor of one church for a third of a century, you've earned the right to a long view. Ronny's personal quest was for significance more than success. He was on a journey toward meaning instead of in a race for numbers. He found a steadying principle in disciple-making, and he followed it consistently.

Do you have a clear belief and commitment that guides you each day and each decade? What's your time horizon for leadership? Do you demand instant gratification from God, or are you patient enough to "wait upon the Lord"?

Purposive Leaders Know the Basic Theological Stories and Their Community's Favorite Story

Purposive leaders understand that, in the larger scheme of life, there are few major themes or scripts for cultures to adopt and live out. Living communities generally follow one of three basic story lines—win-lose, challenge-response, or mature-move.

"Win-loss stories" are obvious in sporting contests and in the classic "cowboys-and-Indians" tales of America's Old West. These stories show up in Scripture in the Persian apocalyptic tradition from the later Old Testament period and the era between the Testaments. Some churches seem to have win-lose emblazoned in their DNA. They appear more confrontational, more brittle, and more schismatic, reactively fighting and dividing over and over again.

"Challenge-response stories" feature a pinch—a provocation, a question, or a dare—and the resolution of the predicament. These stories are fairly common to Eastern cultures, including some of the Old Testament sagas. These congregations face issues as problems to be solved rather than as battles to be fought.

"Mature-move stories" demonstrate the natural unfolding or evolution of cultures where no obvious crisis or apparent threat created an emergency. These stories are teleological in form and are typical of Greek culture. These goal-directed congregations seem to progress steadily toward a goal without many diversions.

Some cultural observers are of the opinion that America's cultural story changed from challenge-response, common to facing frontiers of all kinds, to win-lose after the Civil War when outcomes were viewed as more apocalyptic and catastrophic.

Mission demonstrates a challenge-response story. They had no congregational crisis or threat to trigger change. The malaise was more comfortable, more internal, and invisible. The congregation could have spent another century in its old mode, and it likely would have continued to do well. But, would simply doing well have been the best possible future for Mission? Their response was to accept the challenge when they saw it.

Can you identify your congregation's basic story line? Is your faith community more win-lose, challenge-response, or mature-move in its outlook and problem-solving style? What about you as a leader? Which of these story types have you incorporated into your leader approach?

Purposive Leaders Create Parallel Structures

Reinventing faith communities is messy. The easiest changes to make are the ones that involve doing new things in old, familiar ways or doing old things in fresh, innovative ways. A classic approach to "easier" changes is to develop parallel structures. Ronny began some small groups and launched some mission projects, but he didn't try these outreach efforts at the expense of other groups and mission traditions. We've seen this method. It's the way the United States began.

What can your church do that's new and needed through known channels? What can your congregation do that's tried-and-true but done in new ways? What are some parallel structures you can use?

Purposive Leaders Live by the Maxim, "What You Sow Is What You Grow"

Changed leaders change faith communities. They aren't "managers" of change. They invest in their own growth and in the strategic growth of other leaders. They multiply themselves by planting and cultivating, by appealing for growth rather than demanding or manipulating others to change. I recently heard a young pastor share a "perennial" leadership strategy. He said the way to grow a youth ministry in a church is to begin with five-year-olds and be patient. What you sow is what you grow.

Ronny began his pilgrimage by stretching his own horizons and exploring his own growth. Then, he invited others to join the journey of disciple-making. That's a basic approach for purposive leaders.

Are you taking the risks of germination? Are you ready to invest in the growth of your self and your soul? Are you sowing what you want to grow?

Purposive Perennial Leaders Don't "Go It Alone"

While purposive leaders narrow their message and focus their efforts, they count on the broader community to move forward. The motivating principle is singular, but the manpower is plural. In increasingly complex communities, "co-leadership"[17] is necessary. This theme runs upstream against the traditional concept that leadership is a lonely, individual enterprise. In fact, leadership belongs to the community or institution. Perennial leaders know that fact. Purposive perennial congregations don't risk their futures on the strengths and foibles of any one person.

Who are the leaders—now and next—for your congregation? Who are the teams, groups, partnerships, and coalitions who will shape your church's future?

Purposive Leaders Have Enough Flexibility to Improvise

Purposive leaders distinguish between the "now" and the "next." They have a sense of sequence and a touch for timing. They know when to improvise. They build on the base theme, but they create variations on the theme.

A common image of the community leader used to be the orchestra conductor who blended the gifts of all the players into a harmonious performance. That's not a bad model for leadership—when playing from a pre-written score is timely. In a rapidly changing world, however, the jazz musician is a better image for leaders. Improvisation[18] is needed in a volatile era.

Purposive leaders improvise in full stride. They respond to open-ended contingencies as they appear unannounced. They know God's Spirit moves as it chooses (Jn. 3:8), and so must we.

Purposive leaders improvise within limits. Tradition, time, place, and resources all hem in the options that are open to them. Still, there is grace within the givens of congregational life.

Purposive leaders improvise in the moment. They appreciate the uniqueness of the occasion and are aware of possibilities.

Purposive leaders improvise around mistakes. They have no guarantees of success in leadership. They acknowledge their imperfections and the errors they make. Even so, God redeems their mistakes and uses those mistakes to teach them.

Ronny found there wasn't a pre-written score or set play for calling Mission to be purposive. There were no road maps. Neither were there one-size-fits-all modules to plug in and use. Improvisation was necessary.

Do you know your congregation's basic theme? Can you, and do you, improvise from that baseline? Do you learn when you're "off-key"?

Purposive Leaders Put Their Hearts into Their Leadership

In the older, more stable Industrial Age world, leaders might have led mechanically, by rote. But in our more dynamic and less predictable era, leaders have to put their hearts into their work. These intangibles of the heart include courage and stamina. Ronny discovered that becoming purposive was draining. He had to have his heart in the task to keep on keeping on. The "viewshed" of disciple-making, the vista you can see from a high vantage point, becomes all-absorbing and energy-intensive. As a result, he judged that the sheer energy toll was so immense that he only has one of these purposive pilgrimages in him. Maybe that's the lesson of purposive perennial leaders—becoming single-minded and theologically principled focuses us on a faith community for the long haul.

Do you have your heart and your head in your ministry? Can you hang in for the long haul? Are you cultivating your courage and stamina?

Seeing and Writing History in Advance

Have you ever wished for the foresight to write history before it happens? That's one definition of planning. Ronny led a thirty-member church-appointed vision team who dedicated more than a year to turn the calendar ahead one decade to 2016 in their imagination and create a future scenario for Mission. In the format of an article in the local paper[19], here's what they "saw."

- Early retirement of debt on the 2003 educational building was done to move on to a new building project.
- Construction of the new multipurpose facility for worship, recreation, fellowship, education, and the annual Women's Retreat was completed.
- The new multipurpose building became a community activity center for concerts, programs, and youth activities.
- By 2007, another additional site, a video café, was added as a worship venue.
- A partnership with a local business in Locust launched a coffee shop as an outreach arm of the church, housing workshops on finances, parenting, grief recovery, and other topics of interest.
- Mission teams continued to respond to national and international rebuilding needs, including building long-lasting relationships.
- The scholarship program in Honduras continued to expand.

These many "advances," internal and external, were rooted consistently in the seedbed of disciple-making. Every possibility for 2016 has been evaluated by a basic question: "How does it make disciples?" In the team's future story for Mission, "The more things have changed, the more they have stayed the same. The disciple-making foundation remains intact. There is a spiritual depth to everything the church does. It has not sacrificed quality for quantity. It is the emphasis on developing fully devoted followers of Jesus Christ that has moved the church outside the walls to become 'salt' and 'light' in the world."

Will Mission's 2016 history reflect these expansions in ministry and missions? There are no guarantees in our visions. Even at our spiritual best, we still see only poor reflections in mirrors (1 Cor. 13:12). That's not to discourage us from dreaming. Still, God's horizon is more visionary for us than we can ever imagine. We tend to think in more singular options, while God creates multiple futures for us. But, it will be an adventure to follow Mission as its purposive perennial future unfolds, won't it?

3

Leading Rooted Perennials

Second Baptist Church, Richmond, Va.

DNA Is Destiny—Cracking the Code

Barbara Brown Taylor has it exactly right: "As anyone who studies congregations knows, history matters. The story of a church's birth tends to shape that community's identity for the rest of its life."[1] Roots grow compatible shoots. Even grafted trees reflect their root systems. Their fruit may be hybrid blends, but they always retain the basic DNA from their births. Decades and centuries of change may come and go, but DNA is destiny. Congregational detectives know to trace back to beginnings, down to root systems. Kierkegaard saw a truth clearly: Life can only be understood backwards, but it must be lived forward.

Paradoxically, Second Baptist Church of Richmond may be the youngest old church in Virginia. The congregation's life and growth began in 1820, before the United States had celebrated its fiftieth birthday. Even with nearly two hundred years of ministry already behind it, Second's youthful vigor is striking. How can a church be so young and so old at the same time? The secret is in its roots.[2] Second Baptist's phenomenal root system keeps it perennially young and growing.

Faith, Another Word for Risk

In 1820, Richmond, Virginia, was a small town of 12,000 citizens. The city's population was evenly divided between whites and blacks. Six Christian churches and one synagogue ministered to the religious needs of the citizenry. About 1816, two members of First Baptist Church, Richmond, took a risk. David Roper, a bi-vocational minister working in law and banking, and William Crane, a local leather merchant, followed the example of the Englishman Robert Raikes and began a Sunday school. They taught the Bible, reading, writing, and foreign missions during three evening sessions each week. The larger act of faith, however, concerned their students. They taught young African Americans. Included in the new class were Lott Carey and Collin Teague, both of whom soon pioneered mission outreach in Liberia on Africa's west coast. At first the class met in a place of business on West Board Street. Later, they moved the growing Sunday school group into the balcony of First Baptist's downtown meeting house.

Shortly, the fledgling Sunday school class faced two pressures. First, making slaves literate was outlawed by penalty of fine and flogging. Then, to complicate this educational endeavor even more, First Baptist's pastor, John Courtney, sometimes called "Father" Courtney and a man already in his seventies, insisted on keeping the focus of the Lord's Day on worship alone. He felt the educational efforts of Roper and Crane to teach reading and writing from the Bible were secular desecrations of the Sabbath. After an extended time of prayer and discernment among the lay members of the teaching team, the Sunday school morphed into a new church. On May 5, 1820, the Second Baptist Church was organized. Three prominent ministers preached at the public constitution of the church on July 11, including Luther Rice, legendary Baptist mission agent and colleague of Adoniram and Ann Judson in India.

Second Baptist Church of Richmond was born at the intersection of two acts of faith: bringing literacy to slaves as well as joining the emerging Sunday school movement for Bible teaching. At its birth, Second was both a lay movement and a youth movement. Both were considered risky by the traditional churches. Risk taking was and remains part of the root system and DNA of this congregation. The results of faith-as-risk and an inclusive spirit are evident at many points of Second's life and ministry as a perennial congregation. That faith/risk pattern was part of Second's root system from the beginning.

Getting a Head Start

Why are some congregations more creative and less risk-averse than others? There are lots of possible answers to that question, but perennial plants may offer a fresh response to that question. Perennials, because of their sturdy root systems, get an early start in the growing season. Like sprinters, they are down in the starting blocks at the starting line, primed and ready to burst forward explosively at the first opportunity. And, they do.

When a congregation or organization is clear about its own DNA, it can give life and encouragement to other new entities. Since perennials' roots give them a head start every growing season, Second has also had that knack of the early launch of ministries. Second has consistently seeded and cultivated a broad variety of new ministries. The list below overviews some of Second's impressive ministry yields in three different arenas—leaders in ministries and missions, new ministry places, and religious bodies who partner with churches for "wholesale" ministry locally and globally.

Risking People to People—Ministry Relationships

The array of leaders emerging from Second is impressive. Without noting mayors or business and community leaders, look at the numbers of ministers and missionaries with roots in Second.

- A host of ministers have been called from the membership and ministry of Second. During Second's first 150 years, 34 men are named[3] as entering the Gospel ministry. Others have responded in the ensuing years as well.
- Second called Virginia Withers Harrison, the first female minister in Virginia Baptist churches, in 1930.

Missionaries were sent out and mission societies have emerged from Second. A long lineage of missionaries, mostly to foreign fields, were nurtured and launched from Second. An illustrative list follows.[4]

- William Mylne and his new bride went to Liberia in 1835. Unfortunately, Mrs. Mylne died of a fever only a matter of weeks after arriving in Africa.
- Mary Frances Roper Davenport, the daughter of the founding pastor, arrived in Siam, now Thailand, with her husband in 1836.
- Mattie Hall Chambers and her husband went to China in 1895, and then her sister, Mary Province Chambers and her husband followed in 1904.
- Calder T. Willingham, a son of Second, went to Japan in the first decade of the 1900s. He returned to the United States in 1918 to attend his brother's funeral and also died during the flu pandemic of that year.
- Elizabeth Ellyson Wiley, another child of Second, and her husband went to China in 1921 and remained until World War II broke out. Louise Ellyson journeyed to China to visit her sister in 1923,

married a field missionary there named C. Hart Westbrook, and served with distinction until World War II, briefly returning for another term of service after the war.

- Two missionary nurses, Sallie James and Frances Hudson Vance (with Frances' husband), went to China in 1934.
- Mary Lucille Saunders, born to missionary parents in China, was appointed to service in China in 1939. She later served in the Philippines.

Risking Places—New Launch Pads for Ministry

A similar listing of churches with ties to Second is impressive as well. Among the new congregations encouraged by Second in the early years of its ministry, mostly places still in the heart of Richmond, were the following:

- Third Baptist Church, now Grace Baptist Church, in 1833
- Walnut Grove Baptist Church in 1841, a unique church start in that it was long-distance for the era—eight miles away
- Second African Baptist Church in 1846
- Leigh Street Baptist Church in 1854
- Belvidere Hill Church, now Pine Street Baptist Church, in 1855
- Manchester Baptist Church, later called Bainbridge Baptist Church, in 1857
- Venable Street Baptist Church in 1874

Risking Partnerships—"Wholesale" Ministries

Second has ministered in both "retail" and "wholesale" environments. It has partnered and invested in extensive missions and ministry relationships. Second has been stable enough to take risks. It has used its root system to anchor other ministry agencies. Second has an impressive list of "firsts."

Some of the first-fruits of Second include:

- The Baptist General Association of Virginia. In 1823 the General Association became the umbrella organization for missions, education, and cooperative ministries among Virginia Baptists. The BGAV was organized at Second. Over the nearly two hundred years of the ministry of the BGAV, three members of Second have served as its executive director, and at least nine members have been elected president of the General Association. This pattern of employed and elected leaders is unmatched in Virginia Baptist history.
- Religious Herald. In 1828 the Religious Herald, the newsweekly for the Virginia Baptist family, was founded by members of Second. A member of Second served as editor for the first thirty-seven years.

- University of Richmond. Richmond College, later Baptist Seminary, now the University of Richmond, was founded in the basement of Second in 1832.
- Richmond Female Institute, now Westhampton College of the University of Richmond, was founded in 1854 at the church,
- At the formation of Woman's Missionary Union of Virginia in 1892, its initial meeting was hosted by Second.
- The first meeting and the first office of the Foreign Mission Board, now the International Mission Board, was at Second.
- The first gathering of the Cooperative Baptist Fellowship of Virginia was hosted at Second.
- In more recent years, Second served as a site to test two innovative ministries. At-Home Ministries, an outreach to help aging church members remain in their homes and to age in place, and World Missions Unlimited, a missions outreach ministry, were both piloted at Second.

These outreaches via people, places, and partners multiplied Second's ministry locally and globally—and continues to do so. These lists are impressive "crop yields" from Second's root system. Second has always kept its eyes on the horizon, scanning for more and more ministry opportunities.

Leaders keep their eyes on horizons for possibilities. I recall talking with a campus minister once who told me that he looked out his office window at "a mission field of 25,000 souls." I gently reminded him that his county had another university plus a large community college. His mission field of college students was actually 50,000 souls. He reported that was a sobering moment for him. He discovered that he'd kept his eyes on the lowest horizon rather than the higher one.

Tugging at the Roots

Good history is no guarantee of a good future. Like all churches and other living communities, Second has been tested. The roots and DNA may provide identity and stability for congregations, but that doesn't guarantee endless easy days. Some events threaten to pull the roots out of the ground. At least four events have tested Second's root system.

A Long Crisis, the Civil War

Lyman W. Seeley became pastor of Second in 1857. The church was still young, and Richmond was a growing city. Giving was setting records, Sunday school enrollment was in the mid-400s, and a missions society for city ministries was organized for young men. Then, the United States boiled over on the issue of slavery. In rapid-fire fashion, Virginia seceded from the Union, and the Civil War broke out. Jefferson Davis moved to Richmond and established the city as the new capital of the Confederacy. Richmond's population mushroomed from 38,000 in 1861 to 128,000 in 1864.[5]

The city immediately became an overcrowded and chaotic place. Second, as well as other churches, were impacted in major ways. In the midst of turmoil, the entire church membership contributed to the war effort. Every member of the Young Men's Society joined the Confederate Army. As the younger men members went off to war, the older men and the women contributed, too. They worked to support and supply the army, making munitions, fashioning clothing for the soldiers, guarding prisoners of war, and staffing the fifty hospitals that sprang up. Treating about 16,000 soldiers who were maimed and wounded in the fighting for Richmond was a crisis ministry of the city's churches, including Second. Second's pew cushions became hospital mattresses, and its bell was given to the munitions factory to be melted down for ammunition. Attendance and financial support suffered, but the church persisted in the face of chaos. Seeley resigned as pastor in March 1864. Although the church was greatly weakened, it carried on. The day before Union troops entered the city, Second's Sunday school still had 170 students in Bible study.

Richmond fell to the Union army on April 3, 1865. Retreating Confederate forces set delaying fires to buildings and bridges, leaving many citizens homeless, destitute, trapped, and helpless amid military rule. Military occupation was difficult—there was no money in circulation, no postal service, and few jobs. Making ends meet became everyone's challenge. Second's tithes and offerings for 1865 were only $770. Still, Second cared for needy families, disabled soldiers, and black citizens. The era of Reconstruction was a trying time for the church, but Second refused to give up, and it began to rebuild its life and ministries again. By its one hundredth anniversary, Second had grown to one thousand members.[6]

A Traumatic Loss, a Pastor's Sudden Death

James H. Ivey moved from the First Baptist Church of St. Joseph, Mo., to become pastor of Second in 1945. His ministry in post-WWII Richmond was soon productive. Ivey reached out deliberately to the downtown neighborhood, launched Wednesday night suppers for fellowship and to facilitate meetings of congregational organizations, established a Junior Board of Deacons for men from eighteen to thirty-two years of age, created a board of women to assist the deacons, led in retiring church debt, and founded an endowment fund for the church. Then, just before the morning worship service on February 15, 1953, Pastor Ivey died in his study of a sudden heart attack.

A Tense Test, When Wills Collide

After Ivey's death, the young and less-experienced Owen M. Weatherly served. When he left, the church called its oldest pastor, C. Gordon Brownville, who was sixty-one years of age. The new pastor brought a broad background. He was an attorney in his early work career and then a pastor and evangelist who had served churches from coast to coast. An immediate need for parking for members who attended services faced the church when the new pastor arrived. Brownville pressed immediately to purchase some available property for parking, requested the launch of a radio and television ministry, and appealed for an educational minister. Some building renovations were completed, and offerings increased. Although the church agreed to purchase property for parking, the money to buy the land could not be raised. This turn of fate was a deep disillusionment for the congregation. Brownville resigned in disappointment a month later and returned to his former church in Philadelphia.

A Strategic Decision, the Relocation to Henrico County

Second has "lived" at four addresses through its ministry—11th and Main, 6th and Main, Franklin and Adams, and River Road and Gaskins. Only the final move took Second "out of its neighborhood." In truth, Second's neighborhood had been leaving it for a long while. Business and commercial interests were taking more and more spaces in the city. Residential neighborhoods downtown had been shrinking for several decades. Second's leaders had discussed the loss of participants for a number of years.

Political pinches added their impact. When *Brown vs. Board of Education* mandated school desegregation in 1954, Virginia's politicians countered with massive resistance and closed the public schools. In that polarized atmosphere, many inner city families fled to the surrounding counties. White flight emptied many of Richmond's residential areas. One large inner city church in Richmond's historic Fan District saw half of its members who lived in the neighborhood immediately around their church building move west of the Boulevard into the counties in a single year.

Leaders in uncertain times often ask when the tipping point will arrive. After all, timing is everything in comedy and in leadership. Tipping points, those occasions when change happens suddenly, occur when three streams of behavior[7] flow together. First, ideas and messages can become contagious, spreading quickly and freely in viral fashion. Second, seemingly small actions can have large impacts. Finally, the speed of change escalates dramatically. To miss or ignore a tipping point places communities of faith in jeopardy. Major upheavals in ministry settings such as war; tragic losses such as deaths, fires, losses of key industries and job sources; and major transitions are watersheds for leaders.[8] These challenges are occasions when leaders define themselves or miss the boat.

I consulted with an "Old First" church in the South during the mid-1980s about its future. It was apparent they were fragile, aging, and complacent. After some study and discussion, they decided to do nothing and passively die. I was shocked at their fatalism. Oddly, that congregation knew and admitted they'd missed a tipping point in 1958. At that time they'd considered planting a new church in the suburbs of their growing city. But they'd decided against the new congregational start. The problem they discovered was the idea of a new congregation had become viral, taking on a momentum and romance of its own. The church's younger families and stronger leaders couldn't turn off their dream. They left and established the new church. The remaining members in the original church said they knew fairly soon that they'd missed a key ministry opportunity and were in trouble. They had missed a tipping point. Nearly thirty years later, they sadly recognized their mistake and could not turn back. Their opportune moment was gone.

When Second considered a relocation to the suburbs, it faced several critical questions, the kind of questions that are ultimately a matter of faith.

- Should we merge? Conversations with the Derbyshire Baptist Church and Grace Baptist Church about the possibility of merging took place. Grace had no pastor, and Second had already decided to relocate. But, after a period of discernment, Second determined neither merger option was a fit, and it continued its search for a new site for worship and ministry.
- Can a 140–year-old church become young again? The pastor of one aging and shrinking inner city church preached on the unlikely pregnancy of Sarah, Abraham's wife. Given Sarah's advanced years and applying the situation to his church, the pastor asked, "Can our church 'expect' again?" Was a new day possible?
- Can a church born and bred in the heart of a city make the transition to the suburbs? Second was within walking distance of its hospitals, courthouses, and major businesses. In the suburbs, by definition nothing was within walking distance.
- Can a church with fewer members and resources find strength to grow again? Was the tipping point past?
- Can long-term members and others who have established religious routines develop new habits in their church membership? The question is reminiscent of the story of a first-time visitor who entered an empty church, sat down in a pew, and then heard a regular attender—in the otherwise still empty worship space—say, "Excuse me. You're in my seat." We humans are painfully predictable creatures of habit.

- Can members with a deep appreciation for their classically beautiful worship space in a historic setting move to a multipurpose facility in an undeveloped location? We humans also love spaces. Church members are often accused of having an "edifice complex."

Some Lessons from the Crucible

Second has been a realistic congregation throughout its history. When faced with problems, the members have surveyed the situation in front of them and then pitched in to do what was necessary to move forward. For example, in the midst of the Civil War, Second coped with near-impossible circumstances, survived, and kept reaching out to persons in need. As a current member says, Second isn't a church for "wimps." Second is one of those rare congregations where whatever needs doing gets done. This theme demonstrates itself in a variety of ways:

Second relies on its confession of faith for guidance in ministry and decision-making. It has no other governing documents. What it believes determines how it behaves. The lack of formal documents baffles most churches, but it works for Second, due to the strength, experience, and stability of its members. Relying on lay leaders is an integral part of Second's root system.

Second is a lay-led church. Some observers will scoff at this theme. They know Ray Spence, the recently retired pastor, was a hands-on leader for more than forty years. But the practice of lay leadership has been part of Second's root system and DNA from the beginning. Remember that David Roper, Second's founding pastor, functioned as an unpaid, volunteer lay minister for the first six years of the church's life. Still, Second has a history of unusually well-trained and able pastors, ministers who were very strong leaders and who were partners with equally strong lay leaders.

This pattern is no more obvious than this current moment as Ray Spence moves into his forty-sixth year of pastor leadership at Second. Ray's an influential leader in both Richmond's religious and business circles. Ray has served as president of the Baptist General Association of Virginia, as board member of the Foreign Mission Board, and as founder of the Ray and Ann Spence Network for Congregational Leadership. In the business community, he is the only religious leader to be invited into and to chair the powerful business-oriented Richmond Forum. He has lent his experience to local hospital boards, the board of Collegiate Schools, and has chaired the Fin Fish Sub-Committee of Virginia's Marine Resource Commission. Ray's seen as the best pastor of business leaders in Richmond.

Within the leader mix at Second, he functions like an athletic director for a major university, planning for the next season, coordinating dozens of sports' teams, enlisting coaches for those teams, and keeping the entire team blending its overall strengths for the ministries of the church. It's instructive that Second employs fewer ministers on its fulltime staff than most churches its size, activity level, or complexity. The church relies on its lay leaders for its programs and ministries. And, it always has. Its roots are in lay leadership.

The strength of lay leadership has been most obvious in the "gaps." When the church has been between ministers, facing new challenges, or looking for fresh futures, lay leaders have made the difference. When Pastor Ivey died on February 15, 1953, the church grieved appropriately, arranged for the care of the late pastor's family, elected a fifty-member pastor search group, selected a team of six laypersons to help bridge the emergency created by the pastor's death, and called a new pastor on April 26, 1953, a short ten weeks after Ivey's passing. But the downtown ministry situation was becoming increasingly complex.

The pastoral transition from Ivey to Weatherly was both comfortable and uncomfortable. Owen M. Weatherly, the new pastor, had served Second as associate pastor for a few months already before Ivey's death. He was known to the congregation, providing a measure of reassurance to the membership. Although he was fairly inexperienced in the lead pastoral role, he also knew the congregation and city himself. But Weatherly's challenges were stark. He was following a pastor who died in the midst of ministry, passing away as the membership was literally gathering for Sunday worship. Ministers who become martyrs in death are notoriously difficult to follow.

Additionally, the drip, drip, drip of the losses of decline was now inundated by the traumatic death of their pastor. The church's membership had fallen below one thousand and continued to decline. Offerings had remained flat for several years. Weatherly was able to give hope to the members, many of whom were especially anxious to encourage him as well. He showed concern for the inner city's challenges and joined a number of community organizations. Eventually, Weatherly left Second in 1958 to become pastor of First Baptist Church, Philadelphia, Pennsylvania.

First Roots, Then Fruit

Second Baptist Church in Richmond has been an exceedingly productive congregation since 1820. Their roots have yielded lots of fruit. Second's root system has provided the basic impetus for health and growth. Remember that DNA is destiny. Roots determine shoots. Blooms may be cut and enjoyed in our homes, limbs may be pruned to enhance trees' health, and turf grass may be mowed for a uniform look. But, roots aren't changed. They remain to determine the basic identity and the yield of their plants. The same is true for living communities, such as congregations.

Plants require root systems to survive and thrive. Perennials invest more of their futures in roots than annuals do. That's one reason perennials are so hardy. It's a secret of their success.

Roots Serve Their Plants with at Least Four Primary Functions

Roots anchor and stabilize their plants. Typical of their multi-year development, perennials have especially sturdy root systems. Redwood trees, for instance, are too big structurally for their root systems, so the roots of nearby trees interlace to hold each other up.

The toughness of root systems is deceptive and often missed—until those roots are dug up in transplanting processes. A couple of growing seasons ago, I decided to thin and transplant some decorative grasses in my yard. Many perennials grow from division of the root systems, and, occasionally, gardeners divide their plants for the health of the mature plant and to create new growth. I used a spade to dig into the root mass, but, try as I might, I couldn't dislodge the sections of roots I was trying to transplant. Finally, I used an axe to cut the roots apart enough to move the grass. Above ground, these grasses looked delicate. They flow in the breeze as if they have no weight at all. Their seed plumes are like wisps. But underground those grasses are tough as nails. It's no wonder they're as hardy as they are. They are rooted to survive and thrive.

Generally speaking, plants are made up of root systems and shoot systems, often roughly the same size. Roots are invisible, so we don't think about them. Shoots, however, are out there for all to see. Observed or not, roots are crucial to plant life and health. Without the roots, there are no shoots.

Second Baptist of Richmond is a well-defined church. The congregation is anchored in a clear identity and stabilized by its heritage and strong leaders, both clergy and lay. In fact, lay leadership, a hallmark of Virginia Baptist congregations in general, is especially sturdy at Second Baptist.

Roots find and absorb food and water. Roots provide outreach, searching for resources. In fact, around hardwood trees, roots reach out about three times beyond the area of the leaf canopy. To gather enough nourishment to feed their tree, these roots have to be aggressive and far-flung.

In the search for food, perennials develop two kinds of roots—roots that reach down and roots that reach out. Taproots, or radial roots, grow down. They form thick and long axes, growing deep into the soil for strength and stability. In contrast, fibrous roots grow out. They form tangled networks of branching roots with no dominant root, typical of most grasses.

Second Baptist is resource rich, both in people and heart. The congregation's outreach is phenomenal, both in extent and in depth.

In the affluent West End of Richmond, the church reaches across socioeconomic strata. Second is generous with its resources. Its heritage of caring for persons who are trying to enter society's mainstream remains consistent. Second's roots in ministry to black citizens not only taught slaves to read, it has yielded black churches as well as care for black children and families during and after the Civil War. Currently, Second's English as Second Language program provides a supportive and practical ministry to newcomers to this country. Additionally, Second hosts Russian and Brazilian congregations.

Roots preserve the future. They store essential supplies for demands in the future. In some plants, roots are like cupboards or pantries, holding food material until it's time for stored resources to be transformed and used by the parent plant. Second's view of the future goes back to earlier days.

An unusual aspect of Second's view of the future is its legacy of young leaders. Although it has regularly called on the wisdom of many seasoned and prominent executive leaders in its membership, Second has frequently called young pastors. Six pastors have been in their twenties when they answered the call to Second. The first three pastors were 27 (Roper, the founding pastor), 23 (Taylor, the second and youngest pastor), and 29 (Magoon, the third pastor). Chambliss, the seventh pastor, began his ministry at 26; Landrum, the tenth pastor, was 29; and Ray Spence, the twentieth and recently retired pastor, was 27.

Second retains a young spirit. Across nearly two hundred years of ministry, the vigor and audacity of youth has marked Second. Ordinarily, young pastors are called by churches who are near educational institutions or by churches on the employment margin. Neither is the case for Second. It has chosen to remain a youth movement. Second continues to reach many families and youth successfully.

One of the hallmarks of Second Baptist's view of the future is its debt and funding philosophy. Set on a site that looks like a Southern college campus, Second has funded its recent building projects on 90-day notes. These short-duration payment plans have pressed the church to think ahead constantly and have short-circuited any temptation to become complacent.

Roots hold soil in place. The host soil for plants is held together by the root system of the plants themselves. The partnership between soil and root systems is natural and eternal.

Second Baptist anchors its setting. It's both a neighborhood and a regional church. It touches the spiritual, civic, and business interests of the city. For instance, it offers world-class weekday ministry to children as well as a large-scale recreation program in the community. At the same time, Second hosts the Richmond Symphony for regular area-wide concerts. Its Bread of Life and its Upward Basketball programs both reach out to the community.

Leading Rooted Perennial Congregations

Rooted perennial congregations are unique churches. They know who they are and what their distinctive strengths are. What have we learned about leading rooted perennial congregations? To help set the pace in these special congregations, leaders face several challenges.

Do a "Tissue Match" before Signing on for Leadership in Rooted Perennial Congregations

Even more for rooted perennial churches than for others, faith communities with clear identities and consistent heritages require leaders who match their DNA. In 1992, my brother needed a bone marrow transplant. After testing, it was determined that I was his best match. In fact, we were as alike genetically as twins. Even with our close match and even with powerful medications, the rejection of my marrow by his immune system was a mortal battle. Finally, the marrow "took," and the rejection process was settled.

Potential pastors and new lay leaders are advised to be sure there's a compatible match before trying to guide rooted perennials. Otherwise, rejection is a likelihood. Roots don't negotiate. Richard Southern and Robert Norton call this matching and leading process "growing into who you are."[9]

For Leaders of Rooted Perennial Congregations, Only Grown-Ups Need Apply

Leaders for perennial congregations are required to know who they are. Matching with and leading perennials calls for mature, well-defined persons. Novice adults need not apply, since deep root systems aren't impressed by rootless leaders. Ronald Richardson reminds us, "Defining a self means identifying the beliefs, values, commitments, and life principles on which we will base our lives."[10] For leaders, that's being a rooted grown-up and is a requirement for obedience to Christ and for effective relating in mature churches.

Change in Rooted Perennial Congregations Happens by Extension or Expansion

Some leadership coaches emphasize change, change, and more change. In rooted perennials, change extends and expands core DNA. Fads or change for change's sake don't impress rooted perennials. They respond to new ministries that cultivate and grow from depth, from their basic identity. Altering root systems is risky business and done at leaders' peril, often killing both the community and the leader.

Mary Beth O'Neill describes this process as aligning organizational and personal actions.[11] Leaders function in a context, and they genuinely connect with their community.[12] Then, they show love and appreciation for the healthy aspects of their community and encourage health to flourish.

Leading Rooted Perennial Congregations Is Both Simple and Complex

Rooted perennial congregations are both simple and complex. Although rooted perennial congregations are true to and consistent with their identity, past and present, they are anything but robotic. They have endless richness, diversity, creativity, and even paradox within their root systems. Leading rooted perennial congregations is easy—follow the roots. Leading rooted perennial congregations is complex—get comfortable with mystery.

PART II

Cultivating Perennial Communities

Facing Challenges Head-On

4

Leading Resilient Perennials

St. Mark's United Methodist Church,
Midlothian, Va.

By the Book

It was a textbook beginning. For a church started in the 1960s, the launch of St. Mark's United Methodist Church followed the standard approach.[1] The formula was for an underchurched neighborhood to be identified and then a coalition of denominational and local groups to be gathered. With endorsements from these groups and lots of shoe leather from a faithful corps of members, a launch was planned.

That pattern was followed at St. Mark's. Nine other Methodist churches joined a national organization to found and support St. Mark's as a new mission church. The name for the new congregation was chosen by the New Church Development Committee of the National Board of Missions in Philadelphia before the congregation was formally begun. It was done precisely by the book.

The record of this standard effort is clear:

> On October 15, 1966, approximately twenty men, women and children, under the direction of Rev. Henry Murray, Member of the National Board of Missions, began door to door surveys, general meetings and home social hours to prepare and plan

46

for the establishment of St. Mark's United Methodist Church. This call from God was fulfilled on December 4, 1966, with 26 persons present for a service conducted by Rev. Henry Murray, Bishop Walter C. Gum, and Dr. Purnell A. Bailey.[2]

But St. Mark's is a different church in a different place now. It's been a nomadic journey. The congregation is now a study of perennial resilience. Do you remember that perennial plants have multiple opportunities to be transplanted and repositioned into more favorable settings for them? That's a key to St. Mark's development into a resilient perennial congregation.

A Church on the Move—Literally

Worship services for the little band were initially held in Ferebee's Restaurant on Midlothian Turnpike just west of Courthouse Road. The next year, in 1967, the Richmond District of Methodists first purchased a parsonage in the Shenandoah subdivision off Midlothian Turnpike. Then, about four acres of nearby land along the 9500 block of Midlothian Turnpike were obtained for future development by the church. Services were moved to the Renaissance Theater at Midlothian and Buford Road. Little did the fledgling congregation know that it would eventually have several more worship sites before settling into its current setting on Luck's Lane.

It was time to build. In 1968, plans were finalized, and $65,000 in construction financing was approved by the forty-nine members. Ground was broken, and the church's ministries multiplied to include Methodist Women and two Cub Scout packs. Worship services were moved yet again to Providence Middle School.

The new church building was completed and hosted its first worship service in 1969 for its eighty-six members. A choir was organized. A Methodist Men's group was begun, and Boy Scout, Girl Scout, and Brownie Scout troops were sponsored. By 1971, the membership had grown to 170 members. A music director and accompanist, the first paid staffer, was added to the ministries of the church. Traditions were established. Brunswick stew dinners sponsored by the men and bazaars by the women were popular and successful. Pastor Carl Cofflett instituted the practice of closing worship services by joining hands and singing "God Be with You 'Til We Meet Again." The practice continues to the present day.

Growth was so steady that the original building was remodeled in 1973, and a second service was added. In a major move, St. Mark's opened a nursery school for the community. When the church celebrated its tenth anniversary in 1976, it boasted 300 active members. Outside of a basement that flooded during wet spells and required a shop vacuum to remove the water and to dry out the space, St. Mark's was on its way. Or, was it?

Hitting the Speed Bump

Establishing a church site in a fast-growing commercial corridor was soon to become a two-sided coin. The growth of the community generally benefited the congregation's expansion. But like a python, that growth also began to squeeze the church to death. St. Mark's building was situated back fifty yards from the main thoroughfare in a grove of trees, cozy but more and more invisible as car dealerships and the Groaning Board Restaurant pinched in and shielded the church from easy view. The volume of traffic, often a real asset to growing churches, in this case created a safety hazard as people tried to turn into the church property or leave it. Finances became a pinch point, too. Some members paid their annual pledges from their savings at the beginnings of years. In spite of this depth of commitment and sacrifice, the church lost its momentum and began to lose members as well. It was becoming increasingly clear that the site on Midlothian Turnpike was not a promising place for the church to continue to thrive and grow.

It's a common occurrence for the denominational partners and the local congregation to read the ministry situation on the ground in different ways. Sometimes, the denomination sees looming crises long before the threatened congregation is able to sense it. Sometimes the sensibilities are reversed. It's the old paradox of not being able to see the forest for the trees. In the case of St. Mark's, the church recognized its plight before the denomination could take the situation in. The denomination had always owned the parsonage[3] and still provided a salary supplement for the minister. It was a classic Catch 22 situation. The denomination was, at the same time, both invested and remote. But, the congregation saw its dilemma clearly and made its case to the Methodist structure strongly.

What could be done? Three options were put on the table. St. Mark's could close, merge with Huguenot Road United Methodist Church, or relocate. Of the three possibilities for the future before it, only one was explored actively. Closing the doors or merging weren't considered options. There had to be a better way for the church. Relocation seemed to be the best future.

Failure Is Not an Option

Remember the line in the movie *Apollo 13*, "Failure is not an option"?[4] Flight director Gene Kranz faced the crisis of an explosion on the spacecraft with the conviction that disaster would not happen on his watch. Life sometimes presents us with circumstances that must be resisted. That's what Kranz insisted.

Kranz was a central player in America's manned space program over its first three decades. Becoming flight director in NASA's Mission Control during the Gemini program, Kranz witnessed and helped make history. He directed Apollo 11 when Neil Armstrong fulfilled President Kennedy's pledge to land a man on the moon during the 1960s. In spite of his overall contribution to space exploration, he may be best known for directing the near-tragic Apollo 13 and leading the Tiger Team to find how to get the three stranded astronauts safely back to earth. We remember the event, dramatically retold in Ron Howard's movie, when, on April 13, 1970, Jim Lovell reported, "Houston we have a problem." An on-board explosion crippled Apollo 13. The flight's agenda abruptly did a u-turn, shifting from exploration to survival. We now know that the fledgling space technology failed more often than we knew at the time. In those pioneering situations, the flight crews were left to live by their skills and wits as they did problem-solving literally on-the-fly. In those crises, failure was never an actual option.

That was St. Mark's attitude, too. The need to move was simply seen as a problem to be solved, a challenge requiring a faithful response. Over time, it had become clear that their original site was not a place where St. Mark's could grow into a strong, mature congregation. But, they had a core group of members who had sacrificed to bring St. Mark's to life and to keep it going. This cluster of members was heavily invested in their church and was too closely tied to each other to cut and run. In the face of this challenge, they strongly felt a common purpose in their church. Even in crisis, they felt chosen, blessed, and destined for a better ministry future. Somehow, they sensed, in spite of difficulties, this was their time. Something more and better lay ahead for them. Failure would not be their legacy. When you're down to almost nothing, you're willing to consider almost anything.

The beleaguered congregation stepped out in faith. In the end, they were too resilient to give up and walk away. With God's help, they would find their best future. They were a tightly knit family, communicating fully and easily. They felt their time of ripening had arrived and refused to let St. Mark's die. Like their wandering forebears in the Old Testament, they would endure and cross their congregational wilderness to inhabit their promised land.

And They Lived Happily Ever After—Almost

Most of us want a version of heaven on earth to become the description of our lives, our families, and our places of worship. It's no surprise the perfect fairy tale ends, "And they all lived happily ever after." Since we aren't perfect people, our stories generally aren't that automatic or that simple. Our churches don't always live happily and comfortably ever after.

The early years of the 1980s were challenging times for St. Mark's. The necessity of moving to a better location became clear. It's tough to move young dreams and nearly twenty years of spiritual sweat equity. At one point, they put their church property up for sale, but did not receive one offer to buy. It was a frustrating time for the small remnant.

Then, they reached a tipping point. Typical of tipping points, the speed of change dramatically increased, and a certain contagion for the future emerged.[5] In 1985, two actions happened within a month that closed one door and opened another. Five acres of land were purchased on Luck's Lane, a distance of five or six miles away from the original location, and plans were made to build and move to the new site. Plus, the original church building and property were sold to another congregation.

In that "yeasty" moment in time, a new minister, Glen Evans, arrived. He faced the transition well. On June 24, 1986, he led the congregation of St. Mark's as they worshiped for the final time on Midlothian Turnpike. Characteristic of its early days, the church became nomadic again. The faithful little group of twenty to thirty members began worshiping at the Heritage Child Development Center across from Johnston-Willis Hospital on Early Settlers Road while the new facilities were under construction.

St. Mark's United Methodist Church, Version 2.0

In September 1986, St. Mark's opened their childcare ministry on Luck's Lane and began worshiping on their site in the education building. By Christmas, the new worship center was also ready, and thirty-one families met for the first worship service in the new sanctuary. Like a perennial plant that had been transplanted into more hospitable soil and in a sunnier setting, the church was poised to flourish all over again. A new era had begun. It's almost a truism: perennials respond well to that symbiotic combination of good sun, good soil, and good seeds. St. Mark's Church, Version 2.0 was poised for its debut.

Transplanted into a fresh garden, the church grew quickly and steadily. Just like the well-known realtor's motto, success is often related to location, location, location. On Luck's Lane, St. Mark's found itself in the middle of growing developments, new subdivisions of young families with lots of children. The church was now also located near the Powhite Parkway, a major trafficway that gave easy access to the jobs in the city of Richmond.

Pastor Glen Evans visited aggressively. He was a dynamic and charismatic personality with great ideas, a good manager who brought a business and engineering background to his ministry, and a leader who was strongly goal-oriented. Glen had a knack of finding needed funding at key times, from the denomination and otherwise, for expansions to the parking lot and other projects. Soon, two worship services were offered. By 1991, additional rooms had been added to the education building, and a new fellowship hall was dedicated.

Challenge Is Necessary

Challenge is necessary for persons and congregations to stay healthy. When Columbia University's Biosphere 2 Center was built in Oracle, Arizona, studies were conducted to improve our stewardship of the planet. Inside the 3.1-acre greenhouse and research laboratory in the desert, fruit began falling off the first trees before it had ripened fully. After investigation, a startling fact was discovered. The sealed and protected environment meant the wind didn't move inside as it did naturally outside. The tree's branches, therefore, grew without challenge. Without the wind, the branches didn't strengthen enough to hold the fruit long enough for it to fully mature.[6]

St. Mark's faced the winds of change and challenge. The congregation's sense of being chosen from earlier days was about to bear fruit. Several apparent blockages melted away providentially as the congregation moved forward. What were some occasions of this resistance or challenge for St. Mark's as it relocated?

The Purchase of the Luck's Lane Property Was Unusual

Hubbard Realty was handling the sale of the Midlothian Turnpike property and suggested another site on Courthouse Road. A visit to that site was decisive. The property was located back off the main road, and the drive awakened a "been there, done that" reaction in the trustees. There would be little visibility in this proposed site, a familiar and unwelcome issue already on Midlothian Turnpike. An intuitive decision was made immediately on the spot. The Courthouse Road site was not St. Mark's future.

Then, the realtor proposed looking at another property on nearby Luck's Lane. He warned the trustees that the owner of the second parcel of land had previously welcomed but then rejected offers. He simply hadn't been ready to sell his six acres of land. The trustees went to the second site and liked the potential they saw. The old orchard could be transitioned to fit St. Mark's need. The realtor, who had been chatting with the owner while the trustees walked the land, reported to the trustees that the owner was finally ready to sell. After a brief conversation about whether the trustees had the power to buy then and there, Harry Rast and Phil Shaw decided to pool their resources for earnest money. Each had one $5 bill. They sent the realtor back to the owner with an offer to buy, guaranteed by grand total of $10. To their surprise, the owner sent back a signed contract. Within moments, St. Mark's owned a new church site. They had found their promised land and now had to claim it.

The church members heard the good news gladly. They were ready to move forward. But, Richmond's Methodist District was somewhat less than delighted with the news. They hadn't been consulted in advance, and they doubted the new site was ripe for growth. But, since the die was cast and the contracts signed, the district consented to the move. Now, it was time for St. Mark's to replant itself and see what could grow on Luck's Lane.

The Building Process Was Completed Faster Than Expected

Anyone who's been involved in construction projects dreads delays of deadlines and overruns in costs. That wouldn't be the church's experience. The contractor for St. Mark's new building had just finished a larger project. He moved his entire crew to the new smaller site. As a result, the building was completed ahead of schedule in only six months. Occupancy permits had a way of arriving just in the knick of time. The childcare facility's permit arrived on Friday. The facility housed worship on Sunday and opened to receive children on Tuesday. The same fortuitous sequence happened again in December when the worship center was approved for occupancy two days before the Christmas season's celebrations began.

Moving Was Simpler Than Anticipated

Moves are usually tough to pull off. In this case, two semi-trailers of furnishings and equipment from the old site were packed, transported to the new site, and parked on the back of the new property until the spaces were ready for the stored items. Volunteers to empty the trailers and to put the items in place in the new buildings were plentiful. Even shipments of new equipment, like the interlocking chairs, were on time and in place for opening events.

Finances Were Less Expensive Than Planned

Borrowing money is often a pinch for smaller churches. Several well-timed events helped underwrite the new beginning on Luck's Lane. $50,000 from the sale of the old property provided a down payment on the new site. A friend of a member of St. Mark's made a $10,000 donation to the church. This gift allowed the church to pay its costs for water connections and easements. Additionally, the construction loan was financed with a floating interest rate. The rates fell throughout the building process. When permanent loans were finally arranged, the rates were three points below the original levels. This phenomenon of seeing loan rates decline in the midst of building projects has happened to St. Mark's repeatedly.

Access to the Property Was Improved before the Grand Opening

Remember how access for members and visitors to the old property had become a menace in the latter days of the church's ministry there? That problem was solved in advance and without the knowledge of St. Mark's. While the building construction process was underway, a county transportation official stopped by to announce that Luck's Lane was being widened to four-lanes of traffic.

Even the Trees Seemed to Grow Fast

When an ethos of destiny emerges, a community sees proof of its blessed life almost everywhere. During the early days on Luck's Lane, St. Mark's expanded its parking area. The county inspectors insisted that a barrier of trees be planted as a visual screen. Glen Evans promised the inspectors that the newly planted trees would flourish and grow quickly. And, they did!

When obstacles disappear in the face of faithful risks, we Christians become mystics. It's a proof of the grace of God when challenges are overcome. Such events even remind us that challenge is needed to strengthen us for the productivity we are meant to demonstrate.

Because Nobody Survives Alone

In his fascinating study of animal survival in the hostile elements of winter, the naturalist and science writer Bernd Heinrich explores the elegance of life when extreme conditions reduce life to the sheer struggle to live another day. He mentions that his local part of New England has thirty-eight species of berries. Twenty-nine varieties of winter berries, fruit that remains on the branch through the cold months, provide food for birds when little else is available for them to eat. "Berries and birds are intertwined in an ancient and complex mutual relationship that is as intricate and interesting as that of flowers and bees. This relationship is not always as visible and obvious because it proceeds over time spans measured by seasons rather than minutes."[7] When survival is on the line, most of us need helpers.

Glen Evans recognized the power of St. Mark's "cloud of witnesses," (Heb. 12:1), the impact of an effective helping group. He also saw that none of us survives well alone. After he left the pastorate at St. Mark's, Glen started a nonprofit organization, "Art for Humanity." With a focus on the struggles of the poor in Honduras, AFH's volunteers look for ways "to help the poor to help themselves."[8] These Art for Humanity volunteers deliver one-third of a million dollars in services each year on a budget of only $50,000. No monies are used for overhead, offices, or salaries. Donated items are gathered and given to Honduran families. This organizational model has earned the "Best in America" seal for Art for Humanity, an award showing the highest standards in integrity and accountancy. This award is given to fewer than 2,000 of America's more than one million charity groups.

Art for Humanity has simple goals:

- Clothing and household items are provided for destitute families.

- Necessities—shoes, food, and vitamins—make the difference in the quality of health and of life.
- Homeless families are helped as they build their own homes.
- Poor families are helped as they begin small home-based businesses.
- Basic life needs are met by means of employment.
- Employment also confronts and breaks the systemic cycle of poverty.
- Some of these home businesses are part of the art community in Honduras.
- Microfinancing is the most effective change strategy, one that has impact across generations.
- Poverty-stricken students receive their educational expenses. Some of these young people study art.

The reasons for Art for Humanity's actions are also simple affirmations of faith and human nature:

- The poor typically have more capacity for strength and growth than we may acknowledge.
- The best way to help the poor is not to be too helpful, creating unhealthy long-term dependency.
- Educating the young is the best long-range approach to help the poor reach independence and expand it.
- When we help the poor grow on the inside, we grow spiritually and emotionally ourselves.

This set of beliefs has created a sturdy base of ministry at Art for Humanity and has allowed many Hondurans to begin the process of pulling themselves up by their bootstraps.

In many ways, it's the old "chicken-or-egg" question, isn't it? Where did Glen learn the pattern that became Art for Humanity's helping method? Was it from his experience of guiding the barebones group at St. Mark's as they found a new life, or did he help impart the "second chances are better chances" mentality at St. Mark's and again later at Art for Humanity? In the end, the specific answer probably isn't the key. The outcome is the same. Two communities of faith are both offering futures to others. Both groups, banding together with others, change and enrich lives. Both give second chances, better chances.

Momentum for Ministries and Missions

Following Glen Evans, David Adkins began his twelve-year pastorate at St. Mark's with a congregation with more raw potential than concrete plans. He helped the church find one ministry it could do well and focus on that. In a neighborhood with an average age of thirty-six, youth ministry was an obvious need. With a youth minister, some program money, and some mission projects to do, St. Mark's outreach to youth expanded quickly. By David's final year at St. Mark's, youth ministry was booming. Eighty youth went on a missions trip, and two youth ministers were required to oversee the ministry.

David served St. Mark's through an era of marked growth. As the membership expanded, the cycle of build-and-raise-money repeated itself over and over. Building programs and capital campaigns were necessary to keep from capping the growth potential of the church. Worship services were added, stewardship expanded, and outreach to young families multiplied. It was one of those very rare second chances at congregational health and vitality. As the church grew, its momentum for new ministries grew as well.

"Better Chance" Ministries

Pat Summit, the legendary head basketball coach of the University of Tennessee's Lady Vols, observes that "too many people were born on third base and think they hit a triple. We all stand on somebody's shoulders."[9] In our world, many people are looking for shoulders to cry on, lean on, or stand on. St. Mark's has been a supportive shoulder to its community and world. In some important ways, the church comes by this legacy naturally.

St. Mark's, while not struggling for day-to-day survival any longer, has learned that a band of brothers and sisters is crucial for healthy ministry. In a world where every other person on the planet lives on a daily subsistence of $2 or less,[10] Christians can make a big and basic difference in so many places. Like most churches, St. Mark's looks at local faces first in their outreach and ministries. In its Version 2.0, several of St. Mark's most important ministries are deliberate efforts to provide neighbors near and far with "better chances." It's a commitment that goes back to St. Mark's beginnings, but it also grows out of the congregation's knowledge—from experience—that second chances are often God's best blessings.

The Childcare Ministry

The childcare ministry began early in the life of St. Mark's and continues to be a flagship outreach arm of the church. An early member of the church had a child who needed extensive care, the kind of care that offered respite to families. The church was touched. While the quality and depth of care needed by this particular family wasn't within the reach of the church, the vision of caring for children was born. The program was established and lives on. The very first building constructed on Luck's Lane was designed with the facilities and special building codes for the childcare ministry.

St. Mark's Preschool focuses on the growth of three-, four-, and five-year-old children by:

- creating a relaxed classroom atmosphere
- nurturing warm, individual teacher-child relationships
- emphasizing understanding, guidance, and direction
- providing stimulating experiences, equipment, and toys

The preschool offers an array of learning and childcare programs, ranging from play days for the youngest children to fulltime pre-kindergarten for the oldest children.

The preschool recognizes the multilayered stages and phases of growth three-to-five year olds are experiencing. As a consequence, the ministry intends to make learning a joy and to foster development in several arenas:

- physical development that encourages large and small motor coordination
- social development that demonstrates how to get along with others, blends sharing with independence, and creates a healthy self-concept
- emotional development that cultivates personal security and social coping abilities
- mental development that widens skills in decision making, following directions, and broadening natural interests
- aesthetic development that deepens the appreciation for the beauty that surrounds us
- spiritual development that helps preschool-aged children grow in awareness and understanding God's world

The childcare ministry has a positive reputation and a staff who love what they're doing. Now several of the child workers have more than twenty years of service. At times the donation of the childcare center to the larger congregation has provided an important financial margin. Currently, $700 is still donated each month by the center to the church's budget.

Ironically, this core ministry's leaders originally resisted expanding into childcare, even when a congregational planning task force recommended a broader outreach to working families. Sometimes one success overwhelms other outreach and ministry options.

The Mentoring Program

During David Adkins' pastorate, Peggy White, the principal of the Evergreen Elementary School, approached the church about a site for students in the case of an emergency. The church agreed to offer shelter in the face of crisis. Then, some additional conversations explored how the neighboring school and church might be better partners. The mentoring program was launched. Volunteers responded well. David Adkins jokingly guaranteed "entry into heaven" for those who helped out. Apparently, the members liked the pastor's promise of eternal bliss. The volunteer corps has numbered between twenty and sixty for the fourteen years since. Along the way, pastors have come and gone, a new principal, Joyce Lanier, serves the Evergreen School, and the Providence School has been added to the mentoring efforts. All the while, the commitment to mentoring young people has remained constant. Several of St. Mark's teenagers join the adults of the church in mentoring. This ministry has won a Governor's Award, and David Adkins and Tom Beck have been named Mentors of the Year.

The Faces Ministry

Also during David Adkins' tenure at St. Mark's, the church purchased an adjoining piece of property with a house on it as a youth house. That house now serves as an office for Faces, a ministry to families with children with bi-polar disorder or obsessive-compulsive disorder. This important service was begun by Pat Myers and her husband, who tragically lost a child to suicide and who wanted to prevent such a loss from occurring in other families. The ministry provides support groups, library resources, family assistance, and advocates in court for families who are confronted with emotional disturbances.

20/20 Vision

St. Mark's has had twenty years of ministry in each of two chapters— twenty years of vision and struggle on Midlothian Turnpike and now a bit more than twenty years of vision and growth on Luck's Lane. The growth has been trending upward for most of this second chapter. After another long membership growth cycle that has brought two hundred families into the church and five building programs, St. Mark's has matured and is, as one member described it, "growing into itself."

The church is almost like a family with two "firstborn" children, the phenomenon that occurs when two children are born into the same family but a decade or so apart. The upshot is that each has the blessing, the strength, the destiny that typically accrues to the firstborn child. Firstborns are usually successful and productive.

Look at a fifteen-year sweep of development in St. Mark's ministries:

- In 1991, more classrooms were added to the Educational Building, and a Fellowship hall was built.
- In 1994, the adjacent property was purchased and staff expanded.

- In 1996, the sanctuary, Fellowship Hall, and office space were expanded. The buildings were also connected.
- In 1998, staff was increased again to hire a full-time Director of Christian Education and Children's Ministry.
- In 1999, a third worship service was added, and the role of Director of Music became a full-time position.
- Between the years of 2000–2002, the worship attendance grew to an average of 600, and staff was again expanded.
- In 2003, the Community Life Center doubled St. Mark's space for ministry. A second full-time youth director and more office staff were added.
- In 2004, the Community Life Center was used for worship for the first time, and staff was expanded yet again.
- In 2005–2006, while enriching its ministries to families, youth, and children, St. Mark's began to focus on missions by sending teams around the community and around the world.

There's plenty of momentum at St. Mark's for a long run of resilient ministry at home and beyond.

Leading Resilient Perennial Congregations

Where does resiliency in persons and congregations come from? Some of it is discovered amid hardship, and some of it has to be cultivated. How do leaders develop and practice resiliency?

Adopt a Try-and-Learn Mind Set

Typically, resilient leaders and groups take a matter-of-fact approach to life. When problems arise, they are faced squarely and resolved. Rather than a trial-and-error attitude, resilient leaders and churches use a try-and-learn model. They discover new styles of coping on the fly, and they incorporate blind alleys into their maps for the future. Resilient leaders operate on the assumption that first chances aren't last chances. Thinking historically, industrial leaders have too often bet the farm on the effectiveness and success of a single program or ministry. In contrast, organic leaders keep their options open and let the future unfold as they move forward. They look for creative and flexible ways to meet challenges.

Mix and Match Strengths and Strains

Gardeners know hostile climates or difficult growing conditions require tough plants. So, they choose tough plant materials from the beginning. For example, tundra, volcanoes, and dunes are hostile growth settings. But, even these extreme situations can host adaptable, resilient plants. Extremely hot or cold climates still have a few suitable plants that can thrive. It's a matter of matching the characteristics of plants and settings. The same is true for churches.

Sometimes circumstances create defining moments for us. Crisis, disaster, and hardship are crucible experiences that either make or break cultures, communities, and leaders. Once in a while, we are deliberately exposed to the crucible. Remember the Johnny Cash song about "A Boy Named Sue"? That boy's father gave him a girl's name, knowing that a boy named Sue would have to fight his way through life just to survive. The name was intended to prepare him for and to toughen him against life's onslaughts. In a crucible situation, discipline and focus are required of us. But, that can't be too daunting for believers in Christ who are called disciples, or learners. We are, after all, people who live by discipline. Resilient leaders and congregations learn ways to face difficult situations and match their best resources to the challenges.

Scarred Tissues Are Hardened and Resistant

Have you noticed that scars on your body have tougher surfaces than the surrounding skin and tissues? And, have you noticed that your scarred areas don't bend as easily as undamaged tissues? Our bodies pay a price for trauma and injury. Even if the scars aren't evident to others, those scars are permanent and resistant to changes. Resilient perennial churches like St. Mark's, churches who have faced and overcome near-death experiences, carry the scars of those difficult days, even if those scars aren't visible on a daily basis. The strength it takes to confront difficult challenges generally serves well in crises, but that same strength can also react to future challenges with resistance.

Resilient congregations respond to their challenges strongly and directly. I remember hearing a counselor comment on persons whose personalities are described as "solid as a rock." He pointed out that the advantage of being "solid as a rock" is we are stable and strong. But, he also observed that rocks have a downside as well. Rocks don't bend. That's a head's up for leaders too. Perennial gardeners describe their practice of giving plants three chances in three locations before giving up on them. The flexibility to keep on trying new options finally wanes.

Congregations, like all communities, have a way of becoming more conservative to change over time. The rocklike assets of strength and stability can become a liability when flexibility for new challenges is lost in scarring. Stated in biblical terms, congregational prophets have a way of eventually becoming congregational priests, moving from courage and risk to caretaking and resistance.

Practice Steadfastness

Steadfastness represents a good biblical word. The English term comes from Middle English, meaning, literally, a fixed or rooted place. In

Scripture, God is pictured as someone who can be counted on, constant rather than fickle. Paul's listing of the fruit of the Spirit, including patience and self-control, reminds us that remaining steadily focused is a great attribute of leaders. People, who are by nature competitors and who think in win-lose, do-or-die, now-or-never polarities, are at a disadvantage in a long-term world. They have trouble waiting on God's clarity for the future. Being able to patiently hang in when chaos reigns gives leaders a place to stand.

Readying for a New Growing Season

After a bumpy transition following David Adkins's ministry when worship attendance fell by almost half, St. Mark's is booming again. David Bonney, current pastor, has promising challenges in his second year at the church—the kinds of challenges that bode well for a perennial congregation. Four services are needed to accommodate its regular worshipers. The congregation's financial base is now broad and deep enough that, as one member described it, we "can afford ourselves." New missions opportunities are on the horizon. Congregational morale is positive again. The church is working to assimilate new members and to keep a warm atmosphere. These are the challenges to be faced and solved when you're a resilient church.

5

Leading Diverse Perennials

Bon Air Baptist Church, Richmond, Va.

Born Facing the World

Bon Air Baptist Church was born facing the world.[1] It was from its beginning, and it still is, a "glocal" church, a combination global-and-local congregation. Bon Air's "parent church," the nearby Woodland Heights Baptist Church, had established a practice of generous giving. The church had given birth to new congregations as well as giving 40 percent of its offerings to missions at home and around the word.[2] The neighborhood of Woodland Heights itself was a frontier of Richmond across the "nickel bridge," so named for its toll. Woodland Heights had begun in 1889 as a trolley suburb between the streetcar route of Semmes Avenue and the James River, and its churches felt some of that pioneer daring. Even now, the Berryman Center, a former Methodist church in Woodland Heights, continues to serve a community outreach role, including hosting the Richmond Peace Education Center, the Encore! Theatre Company, and the Vineyards Christian Fellowship.

In May of 1952, Woodland Heights Baptist Church voted to launch a new church in Bon Air. Bon Air was the emerging neighborhood to the south just across the James River from Richmond where moneyed families had earlier summered to enjoy the resorts and the "good air."

The Richmond and Danville Railroad had provided commuter service between Richmond and Bon Air in the early days. The opening of the Huguenot Bridge across the James River to Bon Air in 1948 brought new access and new optimism to the neighborhood. Growth was on its way. As an aside, it's interesting to remember than both communities—Woodland Heights and Bon Air—were "bridge communities" in both geographic and spiritual senses.

Woodland Heights Baptist Church found an eager missions partner in the Virginia Baptist Mission Board and began Bon Air Church with Bible studies, a Vacation Bible School in July, and a Sunday School beginning in August. James Worsham, a seminarian from Woodland Heights, preached at the earliest worship services. When Worsham returned to seminary, another member of Woodland Heights, Edgar Whitlock, filled the pulpit during that first fall.

The mother church and the fledgling congregation wasted no time, however, in calling a permanent pastor. Phil Rodgerson, a native of Norfolk, Virginia, and a pastor in Winchester, Kentucky, was called in September. After completing some unfinished ministry projects from his nine-year ministry in Kentucky, Rodgerson moved to Richmond to begin a thirteen year pastorate. He preached his first sermon at Bon Air on January 4, 1953. This young Ph.D. was a perfect fit for Woodland Heights' legacy in Bon Air. Rodgerson had hoped to teach on the international mission field, but that dream had not materialized. He brought his glocal vision to Richmond and lost no time in helping Bon Air face its new world.

On Rodgerson's first Sunday at Bon Air, twenty-five persons joined the church. Eleven of the new members transferred from Woodland Heights, missionaries in outreach. Growth was steady. Bon Air registered 147 members by the end of 1954. Land was purchased in 1954, a building dedicated in February of 1955, and the church became free-standing and independent in 1957 when Woodland Heights conveyed the land and buildings on Buford Road to Bon Air.

God Bless Everyone—No Exceptions

Not surprisingly, a Missions Committee was established by Bon Air in February of 1958, and its first recommendations were prophetic. Among other stated principles, to remain a missionary congregation Bon Air decided to do more than "pray and pay." Bon Air became a "go-and-do" church. The church didn't choose easy ministries either. It set out to reopen congregations who had fallen on hard times and to deliberately reach out to neglected populations. It later attempted to strengthen its struggling neighbor, Southampton Church, and used community ministry to impact its region.

In many ways, Bon Air determined to leaven its setting for Christ in prophetic fashion. The pattern was made plain when the church decided in August of 1958 not to open a private school if the public schools of Richmond and Virginia were closed to resist integration. It was an emotional time when many churches got caught up in the heat of the moment and lost powerful opportunities to offer Christian witness. A 1970 study committee looked at the school issue again and made the same recommendation—that a grade school not be established at Bon Air. Those decisions show that theological values must guide cultural perspectives. These clear determinations by Bon Air to be active missionaries in (and beyond) the local community have been multiplied many times across the years since.

Bon Air shares one of the key characteristics of perennial plants: their comfort in "mixed meadows." Perennials don't have to be the only flower in the field or to have exclusive rights to a territory. They share and "play well together." In more technical terms, perennials thrive in polycultures of many types of plants rather than demanding to reign in isolated monocultures. The American prairies were typically made up of four perennial grasses or plant types.[3] Diversity fit Bon Air well from its earliest days.

To Be Continued

On May 11, 1966, Phil Rodgerson resigned as Bon Air's pastor to move into a missions leader role at the Virginia Baptist Mission Board. During his ministry at Bon Air, the membership grew from twenty-five to nearly nine hundred, including three hundred baptisms. Across those same years, church property values rose to a half million dollars. In his new denominational responsibility, Rodgerson continued to use his gifts as a missions' innovator.

The exit of a founding pastor can create a loss of confidence and calling for younger churches. But Rodgerson's resignation didn't write "The End" or conclude a chapter in the church in the usual literary sense. Rather, the missions' postscript at that juncture in Bon Air's life reads "To Be Continued."

Bon Air has had four pastors in its fifty-five years of ministry. Continuity has been evident, both in pastoral and lay leadership. Each of these lively ministers has brought gifts that enriched, extended, and expanded Bon Air's central outreach into its community and world. Each of the earlier pastors maintained supportive and constructive relationships with the church.

New Gardeners for the Bon Air Perennial Patch

Bob Cochran, born in Georgia and raised in South Carolina, became Bon Air's second pastor on October 30, 1966. Having served two Virginia Baptist churches previously—First Galax in the Southwest and Del Ray, Alexandria, in Northern Virginia—he understood the general ministry context in Richmond. During Cochran's twenty-year pastorate at Bon Air, membership increased from 880 to 2244 with 1020 baptisms. Bob's early life had been challenging. One of his college jobs was working at the city jail in Columbia, South Carolina. Soon, he was preaching five services each Sunday in the jail, with separate services for men and women, for blacks and whites, and for police officers. During Bob's ministry at Bon Air and with his blessing, Bob Smiddy, Tom Parlette, and Larry Prentice launched a strong and continuing prison outreach in 1978. Additionally, the church started sending lay teams on international partnership trips and launched the English as a Second Language ministry in 1983.

Jim Pardue, a Louisianan by background, answered the call to become Bon Air's third pastor in 1988, moving from the First Baptist Church of Clinton, North Carolina. The search team had realized that Bon Air had become a regional church rather than a neighborhood congregation, and they looked for a new pastor who could serve regionally. Jim was a seasoned minister with broad experience in missions work and with different church types. He set out to build on Bon Air's sturdy foundation. During Jim's tenure, a Sunday School attendance record of 996 was set in 1990, a second morning worship service was launched in 1991, two major building projects were completed in 1992–93 and in 1999–2000, Upward Basketball was begun, and a ministry to internationals was established.

Travis Collins, an Alabama native, came to Bon Air from Kentucky as Bon Air's fourth and current pastor in June of 2002. Travis had served abroad as a missionary professor at the Nigerian Baptist Theological Seminary in Ogbomosho. His hobby takes him into the community to officiate football games. During Travis' pastorate, the church's trend of numerical growth and transformed lives has continued, the James River campus has been established as a video site, and community ministries have been expanded.

Cultivating More Than a Half Century of Missions Momentum

What combination of leaders and ingredients has given Bon Air fifty years of health, vision, and courage? The characteristic of perennial plants of thriving in "mixed meadows" is evident at Bon Air. Several factors have helped the congregation deal creatively with its diversity:

Risking from the Middle

Bon Air's decision-making style emerged early and has remained uniform across the years. The church has practiced "all" decision-making:

- *all* the information that's available
- *all* the time needed for discernment
- *all* the members gathered in a fair forum

The pattern of going with a solid majority and using established structures has served the church well. Broad-based decisions have provided a springboard for ministry action. When the congregation hasn't given careful study to a decision, the results haven't been as productive.

One approach Bon Air has used flexibly is the trial run. For some new or unproven ministries, the congregation has adopted a "let's try it and see how it works" experimental style. NorthStar Community is a pilot that worked and continues. Bon Air's Saturday Night Contemporary Service was a pilot that worked for two years, then lost its momentum, and was discontinued. Bon Air is grounded enough in its mission calling to evaluate a ministry trial, be sure the yield is worth the expenditure of time and resources, and determine whether or not to continue.

At times Bon Air has had disagreements and official church conferences have been tense. Debate is part of Bon Air's style of decision-making. In fact, when Huguenot Road Church was begun, some members who had spoken forcefully in church conferences chose that opportunity to go with the new start.

Living under a "Big Tent"

Travis Collins describes Bon Air's willingness to take risks in ministry and missions as "creative traditionalism," the knack of seizing the future from basic theological convictions. Bon Air offers five different giving plans, allowing members to choose how their tithes and offerings are used in ministry. The church's broad diversity is apparent in the ability to affirm women in ministry while fostering conservative social positions, doing aggressive evangelism while espousing the separation of church and state, and allowing members to be various congregations within one family, or, as one member described this style, having "one foot in two boots."

Relying on the Continuity of Lay Leaders

Some lay leaders' names appear again and again in Bon Air's breakthroughs. Charter members such as George Warriner, Lois Francisco, and Janie McDorman have provided key leadership. Bob and June Bass are also prominent leaders. Joining in 1958, they immersed themselves into the life of the church. Bob has served as the moderator of the congregation for more than thirty years. Dick Bidwell has been a key contributor both in Bon Air and the larger Baptist family. Frank Voight, a staffer at the Virginia Baptist Mission Board, is credited with keeping a strong emphasis on outreach through the Sunday school and for identifying youth musicals as a primary approach to involving and recruiting young people. Buddy Gardner has been intensely involved in Bon Air, including chairing the most recent pastor search process. Bill Harrington provided leadership in establishing the James River campus. Other lay leaders could be noted if space allowed. Scores of youth and young adults have emerged from Bon Air to serve as ministers and missionaries. Some members now fret that the reliance on lay leaders may be waning at Bon Air in the face of the size and complexity of the congregation's life, a natural growing pain from expansion.

Using Well-led Transitions to Open Doors to "Next Step" Ministries for the Congregation

Bon Air has dealt with their ministry transitions wisely by choosing ministers who have fit each emerging age and stage of the congregation's life. Phil Rodgerson was the birth parent, Bob Cochran the boom leader, and Jim Pardue the builder. Now, Travis Collins is the bridger to new opportunities. The handoffs from pastor to pastor have been smooth, similar to a well-coordinated relay team. The affectionate admiration of all the pastors for each other has added to the faith journey of the church.

Additionally, Bon Air has issued clear calls to their pastors and staff ministers with the future in mind. The church was sure and affirming enough of Maurice Graham as an associate minister that they waited two years until 1991 for him to return from Kuwait after Desert Storm. In Bon Air's entire history, only one minister has been dismissed. One staffer, Paul Honaker, has served in music ministries for more than a third of a century.

One of the untold stories of Bon Air is the giftedness of the pastor's wives. Bernice Rodgerson served as the church's first choir director. Jo Cochran, a skilled educator, taught a nine-year-long biblical survey course with her husband. Judy Pardue began the Rainbow Class, a learning opportunity for persons with disabilities. Keri Collins, a nurse, launched a Monday Bible study for an interested group. The pastors were matched in moving the church toward "next challenges" by their wives.

Travis Collins described the search team who identified him as the fourth pastor as being "regular church." They clearly represented the church and accurately described it. Sometimes churches sabotage their futures by choosing search teams who have too many special interests and miss the mainstream dreams of the congregation. Bon Air has wisely selected leaders—both lay leaders and clergy leaders—who understand the past, are anchored in the present, and see the future.

Maintaining a Consistent Vision of Mission Outreach

Bon Air has been blessed by God for serving populations that will never see the inside of the church. English as a Second Language, the prison ministry, and working with Caritas, a Richmond-area ministry to homeless persons and families, are examples of creative and consistent mission work. Bob Bass describes Bon Air as "always exciting and a fun place to belong."

Ministry—in the Middle, on the Margin

Some churches do missions and ministry in the hearts of their communities. Others choose to work on the margins. Bon Air has done both. With their core commitment to community outreach, Bon Air has leavened the region in many ways, especially through four mission initiatives: prison ministry, recovery ministry, community ministry, and multi-site ministry.

Risking Ministry in Prisons

In Jesus' sheep and goat judgment story (Mt. 25:31–46), a clear principle of kingdom faithfulness is stated. To those who were blessed in judgment, Jesus affirmed, "I was in prison and you came to visit me" (25:36b). Bon Air has taken that plain teaching seriously.

In the late 1970s, Tom Parlette, a prison warden at the Powhatan correctional facility and a member at Bon Air, opened the door to the church for a prison ministry.[4] Pastor Bob Cochran, with his experience in jail ministry and his commitment to evangelism, encouraged this outreach effort immediately. Soon, a new member, Larry Prentice, took the lead. Larry's faithfulness and doggedness kept the ministry going.

The need was and is acute. Virginia has slightly more than forty prisons and correctional facilities with 37,000 inmates. More than 41,000 inmates are anticipated by 2011, a population larger than Virginia's cities of Charlottesville, Blacksburg, or Leesburg.[5] With the leadership of Garry Sims and forty volunteers, Bon Air's prison ministry now reaches out to nearly twenty of these crowded facilities. Garry's salary is paid by Bon Air, and other congregations help with other costs and other aspects of the ministry.

Bon Air's prison ministry provides worship services, Bible studies in both on-site and correspondence formats, and discipleship courses by correspondence for new Christians and believers who are ready to grow in their faith. Additionally, music programs, gifts of teddy bears and toys for the children of inmates who come to the prisons on visitation days, and Christmas cards to inmates in Bon Air's programs are also furnished.

One prisoner who received a Christmas card in 2006 wrote a grateful poem to the church:

'Twas the night before Christmas,
in this cold prison jail,
and I stood by my cell door,
praying for mail.

I thought of presents and carols,
as the mail-guard drew near,
hoping someone would remember me,
on Christmas this year.

I thought of those Wise Men,
who brought gifts to that manger,
but all I wanted was a card,
from a friend or a stranger.

God gave His own Son, to set people free,
to teach us to love, even prisoners like me,
and on Christmas, and every day, we shouldn't forget,
there are all kinds of prisons, and it's not over yet.

I was standing there thinking, when the guard finally came,
and when he said the number that follows my name,
the Spirit of Christmas, warmed the cell with pure care,
when he handed me a card, sent with love from Bon Air.

I smiled for a moment, though no one could see,
and I thought of the prisoners waiting like me,
for somebody somewhere, to show Christmas love,
that's the reason why Jesus was born from above.

Bon Air's prison ministry has a number of challenges before it now:

- networking more churches to enrich prison ministries across the state
- providing more guidance to prisoners who are transitioning back into their communities
- supporting more ministries for women and juveniles
- lobbying political structures for more education and faith-friendly options for inmates

Risking Ministry to Persons with Hurts, Habits, and Hang-Ups

Bon Air took a big step in community missions when it reached into unknown territory and established an addiction recovery ministry.[6] In the fall of 1998, Bon Air's associate pastor, Maurice Graham, proposed the exploration of a new ministry based on Saddleback Church's Celebrate Recovery model. The church had sponsored support groups earlier, but none of these groups had lasted. In February of 1999, the ministry now called NorthStar Community[7] was launched in a "safe" setting, the Bon Air Elementary School, only two blocks from the central Bon Air campus. Typical of Bon Air's mission pattern, the ministry was begun as an eight-week pilot program. It has thrived for eight years already.

That's not bad for trial run. But, Bon Air has often "tried on" ministries to test the fit.

Recovery ministries are notoriously difficult for churches. There's no "cheap grace" in successful recovery. For one thing, persons who are in recovery are dealing with some of life's most painful and persistent experiences—unresolved grief, depression, divorce and broken families, legal and court-related challenges, anxiety, and dissatisfaction with life's circumstances. Additionally, these issues are often complicated by coping styles that are marked by rigidity, rituals of habitual behavior, insecurity, shame-filled reactions, fear of failure and abandonment, and underdeveloped approaches to emotional and spiritual threats. Bon Air took a realistic look at the needs and saw ways to reach the recovery population with a distinctively Christian spirit and message.

NorthStar Community envisions itself drawing all hurting people back to God through Jesus Christ. That vision acknowledges that spirituality is messy today. We live in a broken world, and we contribute to that general brokenness with our own broken relationships, broken families, broken promises, and broken dreams. Recovery begins with us admitting that most of us are recovering from something—overworking, overeating, or overspending; perfectionism, codependency, or destructive relationships; fear, anxiety, guilt, anger, or insecurity; or gambling, abuse, or lying.

Mending such pervasive brokenness demands broad and creative initiatives. NorthStar Community focuses on the "3 R's"—recovery from addictions, relational health, and renewal by means of twelve-step programs, support groups, and a variety of publications. The original leadership team consisted of twenty members from Bon Air. The core leaders across the span of years of NorthStar Community have been Teresa and Peter McBean as well as Bugsy and Sue King. Teresa is the public face of the community on its television program and in other settings, but she works with the NorthStar Community team. Teresa has been a member of Bon Air for thirty years, arriving as a newlywed with meager church background who found a new family in the Sunday School classes and training programs of the church. In Bon Air, she found such love and encouragement that she now tries to replicate that quality of care in her NorthStar ministry. Teresa studied psychology at the University of Virginia but arrived at the conviction that God was more apt to heal human brokenness than psychological therapy was. She immersed herself for five years in Scripture and lay ministry at the Christian Counseling Training Center, a nondenominational outreach in downtown Richmond sponsored by Needle's Eye ministry. Teresa affirms that passion without preparation often leads to ministry wreckage.

With the good work of Teresa and the NorthStar Community team, the ministry operates on some basic principles:

- Community is necessary for freedom from hurts, habits, and hang-ups.
- Addictions are spiritual problems and require lay communities of fellow wounded healers to break the addictive patterns.
- The constant, intimate contact of spiritual friendships offset addictive behaviors, which is why NorthStar has expanded to two worship celebrations to limit group size to fewer than two hundred persons and offers 24/7 access to persons in recovery.
- Spiritual accountability is central to the recovery community.
- Dialogic teaching draws participants into learning and applying biblical principles.
- Predictable, consistent patterns of involvement and systematic teaching and programming comfortably fit the addictive mind.
- Failures are a natural part of life. Learn from them, and move ahead redemptively.

One of NorthStar's most powerful offerings is its "12 and 12" program, offering a Christ-centered approach to the traditional twelve-step program in twelve months. The twelve-step principles from Alcoholics Anonymous have been adapted and then undergirded by Scripture:

1. We have admitted that we were powerless over our dependencies—that our lives had become unmanageable.
   "I know that nothing good lives in me, that is, in my sinful nature. For I have the desire to do what is good, but I cannot carry it out" (Romans 7:18).
2. We came to believe that a power greater than ourselves could restore us to sanity.
   "It is God who works in you to will and to act according to his good purpose" (Philippians 2:13).
3. We made a decision to turn our will and our life over to the care of God as we understood him.
   "Therefore, I urge you, brothers, in view of God's mercy, to offer your bodies as living sacrifices, holy and pleasing to God—this is your spiritual worship" (Romans 12:1).
4. We made a searching and fearless moral inventory of ourselves.
   "Let us examine our ways and test them, / and let us return to the Lord" (Lamentations 3:40).
5. We admitted to God, to ourselves, and to another human being the exact nature of our wrongs.
   "Therefore confess your sins to each other and pray for each other so that you may be healed" (James 5:16a).
6. We were entirely ready to have God remove all these defects of character.

"Humble yourselves before the Lord, and he will lift you up" (James 4:10).

7. We humbly asked God to remove our shortcomings.

"If we confess our sins, he is faithful and just and will forgive us our sins and purify us from all unrighteousness" (1 John 1:9).

8. We made a list of all persons we had harmed and became willing to make amends to them all.

"Do to others as you would have them do to you." (Luke 6:31).

9. We made direct amends to such people whenever possible, except when to do so would injure them or others.

"Therefore, if you are offering your gift at the altar and there remember that your brother has something against you, leave your gift there in front of the altar. First go and be reconciled to your brother; then come and offer your gift" (Matthew 5:23–24).

10. We continued to take personal inventory and, when we were wrong, promptly admitted it.

"So, if you think you are standing firm, be careful that you don't fall!" (1 Corinthians 10:12).

11. We sought through prayer and meditation to improve our conscious contact with God as we understood him, praying only for knowledge of his will for us and the power to carry it out.

"Let the word of Christ dwell in you richly" (Colossians 3:16a).

12. Having had a spiritual awakening as the result of these steps, we tried to carry this message to others, and to practice these principles in all our affairs.

"Brothers, if someone is caught in a sin, you who are spiritual should restore him gently. But watch yourself, or you also may be tempted" (Galatians 6:1).

NorthStar leans on other ministries for encouragement. During the early years, Saddleback was the model. Now, along with ten other churches, NorthStar meets twice each year with the Leadership Network to explore new ministry options for recovery outreach and to recharge spiritual batteries. But the basic support network for NorthStar remains Bon Air.

NorthStar's outreach continues beyond its immediate recovery community. It has established many ministries:

- a nonprofit organization to publish materials and to coach other churches who are considering or beginning recovery ministries
- a weekly television ministry
- a Web site for outreach
- a feeding ministry
- a prison ministry through which 430 inmates are going through a twelve-step process
- a partnership with a treatment center in downtown Richmond

Risking Ministry in Multiple Sites

While Bon Air has continued to grow at its original campus, it has also attempted traditional church starts at the Huguenot Road and Woolridge Road missions. Additionally, it took on the difficult task of stabilizing and aiding its faltering neighbor, the Southhampton Church. Along the way, Bon Air donated $5000 to the fledgling Swift Creek Mission. These processes are a natural outgrowth of the legacy of Woodland Heights, Bon Air's parent church.

Bon Air had offered off-site ministries at NorthStar and Southampton. But, at James River, Bon Air attempted a new thing. On September 24, 2006, Bon Air launched a new multi-site ministry:[8] its James River Campus in suburban Midlothian, with John Sawyer as site pastor.

Typically, the recent multi-site phenomenon launches many congregations from one campus, generally using satellite and video resources. This approach to congregational multiplication has at least ten advantages:

- Offers the strengths of larger churches with the intimacy of the small congregation.
- Blends a congregation that's brand new with a known and trusted brand.
- Combines ministry staff generalists and specialists.
- Joins the resources of a stable congregation with the impact of new ventures.
- Multiples new church energy with the resources of a large congregation.
- Unites the momentum of a new location with an established site.
- Calls fresh and seasoned leaders into new challenges.
- Links the natural outreach opportunities of new churches with mature faith of more experienced Christians.
- Builds on the historic value of missionary outreach in a ripe mission field.
- Anchors theologically in the abundance of the "both-and" of the Gospel rather the scarcity of an "either-or" mind set.

The James River site centers in worship and small groups. A newcomer's luncheon provides basic information about the church, including its mission, vision, and membership requirements. Additionally, a "Joy of Belonging" class gives orientation to the values and beliefs of Bon Air as a discernment process for potential members. Small groups in homes invite persons into fellowship and learning relationships. Future sites across the Central Virginia region are being considered now.

Risking Community Ministries

Currently, Bon Air's community ministries are led by a gifted African American woman minister, Valerie Carter. Valerie has experience in inner city ministries and statewide missions programs. Bon Air offers a dizzying menu of community ministry options for members and volunteers from beyond the church. A variety of these ministries are noted below:

- English as a Second Language has been offered for nearly twenty-five years. Eloise Price, a longtime member and former children's minister, coordinates this basic program.
- Hope Resources is a multi-housing ministry with a unique history. When the church attempted to begin a ministry to the Suburban Mobile Home Village a number of years ago, they discovered the village only allowed residents to provide religious services. Under the leadership of Noreda Morgan, Bon Air looked at the potential of this outreach, organized a not-for-profit organization, bought a mobile home in the Village, put a member family in the facility, and launched the ministry. This ministry continues and may become another multi-site location with an emphasis on reaching Hispanics.
- A Hispanic church is part of Bon Air's home campus outreach. A Japanese school meets at Bon Air on Saturday mornings, and a Korean congregation uses space there, too. An international Bible study is part of the James River campus ministry.
- Several medical services are provided within the community. In partnership with Bon Secours Health System, uninsured children and adults can see a doctor, have a physical examination, and receive immunizations. Additionally, Bon Air's parish nurses assist members with health and wellness issues, and seminars, such as The Great Physician's Rx for Health and Wellness, are offered.
- Outreach to homeless and hungry populations is extended through club activities and food pantries.

Mission outreach from the middle and on the margins has characterized Bon Air. The four ministries profiled above are prominent ministries of the church, but they are only a sample of Bon Air's heart and hands. Its leader corps has sustained the diversity of the congregation for more than a half-century and shows no sign of narrowing its horizons.

Leading Diverse Perennial Congregations

Diverse perennial congregations call for unique leaders. Thriving in mixed meadows, diverse congregations find ways to minister well in differing settings and cultures. What do leaders of diverse perennial churches do to be effective in "mixed meadows?"

Avoiding Culture Blindness

Leading faith communities in a multicultural world is more nuanced and more difficult than leadership was in unipolar settings. The church growth movement's "homogenous growth principle" observed that gathering members from the same backgrounds and from the same lifestyles made for the easiest and fastest church growth. That's true. Birds of a feather do flock together. That's both a folk saying and a fact of communal life. But that principle neither reflects the emerging church in the early chapters of Acts nor contemporary cultural trends. Our world is simply more diverse. And, our leaders are called on to move deftly and comfortably across dissimilar communities. That's not easy for many leaders. It requires more strategic and nuanced thinking and acting than some leaders can easily manage. Nevertheless, congregations and ministry settings are naturally becoming more complex and diverse than ever before.

Bon Air has always had a contingent of members who are staff missionaries at the Richmond Baptist Association, the Virginia Baptist Mission Board, and the International Mission Board. Additionally, members from Bon Air have answered the call to volunteer and career mission service. The missionary vision has led to sponsoring Vietnamese families, establishing a strong program in English as a Second Language, and planting a variety of churches. Bon Air has 20/20 culture vision and sees its world through both local and global lenses.

Mary Catherine Bateson poses a telling question for today's leaders: "What would it be like to have not only color vision but culture vision, the ability to see multiple worlds of others?"[9] For Americans who have somehow "successfully" avoided multicultural connections, the most recent census results show that Hispanics, African Americans, and Asian citizens make up one-third of the population of the United States. Muslims now equal Jews in numbers in America. With China and India emerging as global business powers, the diversity of the world is guaranteed. Leaders who become blindly locked into a "Not invented here" mentality will doom themselves to obsolescence. They will demonstrate culture blindness.

Ministering with Excellence and Staying Consistent

A recent study of church growth in more than five hundred Presbyterian churches found some intriguing trends. In a denomination that's otherwise generally declining in numbers, some congregations are thriving. In these congregations, three characteristics[10] are evident:

- Lay leaders are empowered and authority is shared.
- The congregation reaches out for new members, welcomes entering members, and deliberately incorporates them into the mainstream of the church's life.
- Ministries are focused on children and youth.

The Presbyterian profile reflects the ways Bon Air has done its ministry, too. Bon Air has consistently empowered laity, involved new members, and reached out to children and youth.

Risking Expands with Diversity, But Faith Expands Too

Risk is the secular term for faith; faith is the religious word for risk. They go together in ministry. They are multiplied when ministry becomes more diverse. Bon Air has exercised great faith in such ministries as its prison outreach and recovery program. Risk-averse leaders aren't productive matches for congregations who expand the diversity of their ministries.

Leading Leaders

Bon Air and other diverse congregations depend on strong, energetic, persistent, and motivated leaders in many arenas. Leaders in these settings must be comfortable with complexity. Great credit is given by Teresa McBean to Travis Collins, Bon Air's current pastor. She notes that recovery ministries live on the precipice of disaster daily as high-risk communities with vulnerable constituents. Knowing that Travis supports the ministry in all its messiness and prays for it gives Teresa and the other leaders of NorthStar Community the heart and faith to go on. Actively encouraging and aggressively resourcing—from some distance—are marks of the core leaders of diverse perennial congregations.

Thriving in "Mixed Meadows"

Perennial plants do well in mixed meadows, growing well with other compatible plants. So do perennial churches. Bon Air models an uncanny ability to work in diverse ministries and, more importantly, to create them.

6

Leading Flexible Perennials

Brandermill Church, Midlothian, Va.

Birth Parents for a Special Church

Twenty-five pioneers met on January 16, 1977, to form The Brandermill Church. Few Christians have the opportunity to be midwives in the birthing of a new congregation, parents in the maturation of a faith family, and grandparents of a mature church. Brandermill is blessed to have 23 percent of its 120 charter members from those days of new life, participating still after thirty years of active ministry. The neighborhood church they began in a planned community nearly one-third century ago has now grown into a regional ministry center.

Brandermill Church is a "both-and" congregation, both Presbyterian (PCUSA) and Methodist (UMC).[1] To Presbyterians, Brandermill is technically a "Union Church." To Methodists, Brandermill is a "Cooperative Ecumenical Parish." To both denominational families, Brandermill is a living expression of the unity of Christ's universal church. In practice, Brandermill operates as an interdenominational congregation. It's been rightly described as a special church that has been "difficult to peg."[2] Tough to describe or not, this flexible venture in congregational planting has succeeded. Brandermill is the largest of PCUSA's 177 union churches, with nearly 1200 members.[3]

In the plant world, perennials are characterized by a variety of beginnings. Some perennials grow from bulbs, others from seeds, some from transplanting new plant sets or by dividing overgrown plants, and others from rooting cuttings from mature plants. There's no single "right way" in the perennial universe to launch promising new starts or productive cycles of future growth. This same flexibility applies to congregational life as well, especially to Brandermill Church. "Both-and" churches, or blended family congregations, learn quickly to maintain variety, balance, and creative tensions.

Church by the Lake

Brandermill Church is located in Chesterfield County,[4] 446 square miles of old history and new expansion in Central Virginia just across the river from Richmond, the commonwealth's capital city. This bustling county is virtually surrounded by water—the James River to the north and east, the Appomattox River and Lake Chesdin wrapping around from the west to the south and east, and the smaller Swift Creek Reservoir in the northwest sector. Brandermill, on the shores of the 17,000-acre Swift Creek Reservoir, is a natural site for a "church by the lake."[5]

Suburban Chesterfield County and its more than 300,000 citizens boast many historic firsts from colonial days to the present:

- the first site of scientifically cultivated tobacco at Bermuda Hundred (1612)
- the first incorporated town in America and the home of John Rolfe and Pocahontas, Bermuda Hundred (1614)
- the first iron furnace in the New World at Falling Creek (1619)
- the first lead mines in America at Falling Creek (1621)
- the first American hospital, Mount Malady, near Dutch Gap (1622)
- the first commercially mined coal in America in Midlothian (1709)
- the first paved road in Virginia, the Midlothian Turnpike (1807)
- the first deaf school in the United States at Cobbs (1812)
- the first railway in Virginia, the Midlothian to Manchester Railroad (1831)
- the first national Father's Day observation at Drewry's Bluff (1921)
- the first wayside park in Virginia at the Old Stone Bridge over Falling Creek (1934)

As the northwestern quadrant of Chesterfield County grew in the middle decades of the twentieth century, a planned community of small neighborhoods was begun in Midlothian along the eastern shore of the Swift Creek Reservoir. Brandermill grew according to plan quickly, now numbering about 3,000 homes. By 1974, there was talk of establishing a church in the Sunday Park section of Brandermill, near the lake. The developers created a chain of smaller, distinct neighborhoods within the larger community. A community church was seen as a way to grow religious and civic bonds within the diverse and distinctive development. The opportunity for ministry as an agent of community building was there in Brandermill. So was the interest. The pioneering image among the new homeowners would serve the new church and community well.

A Flexible Beginning

Residents of the community approached the Virginia Council of Churches about beginning a congregation.[6] The Council formally proposed the launch of an ecumenical church in Brandermill alongside Swift Creek Reservoir. A number of denominations considered joining in. Three groups, including the Christian Church (Disciples of Christ), were willing to endorse and support the church planting enterprise. But only the Presbyterians and Methodists had available funds to contribute to the beginning of the new congregation. The chemistry between the two sponsoring denominations was enhanced by an unusual fact—the local Presbyterian and Methodist officials, Reverend Sam McCammon and Reverend Harry Eaton, had been friends at Union Theological Seminary in Richmond and were comfortable with and trusting of each other. Possibly, Brandermill wouldn't have seen the light of day without their relationship.[7] It is likely that neither denomination knew what Brandermill would become. As hybrid creation, the church didn't conform to the polity and structures of either denomination, so both sponsors provided extra latitude and let the process unfold.

The two denominational groups moved ahead with plans. Reverend Clyde Bartges, a Presbyterian, was agreed on by both denominations as the organizing minister. The developing company allowed its real estate sales office, or Reception Center, in Sunday Park to be used as an informal meeting place. Within two months, worship services and Sunday school were begun. The first communion service was observed on Palm Sunday of 1977, and a new tradition honoring each denominational family's practices was established—both grape juice and wine were offered in the sacrament. On the next Sunday, 150 worshippers gathered for the first celebration of Easter for the fledgling congregation. The service was held outdoors on the peninsula by a large pavilion overlooking the lake, and fresh daisies were presented to worshipers as they left the event to return to their homes.

During that first summer, worship services were conducted on the deck outside the Reception Center. In the fall, services moved inside the Windward Watch Restaurant. These early experiences of outdoor worship encouraged the growing congregation to preserve an interactive atmosphere, later incorporating seating in the round and exposed beams in their first building. Basic ministries were established early. Sunday school, a music program, and Boy and Girl Scouts were organized by strong lay leaders. The church had a warm neighborly feel and provided a sturdy religious base for the community.

A covenant for a union church was developed by both of Brandermill's sponsoring denominations. A judicatory steering committee was formed for the church, consisting of three representatives each from the denominations and from the church. The steering committee's responsibility was to formulate and work toward common goals and to aid communications. To maintain balance over time, it was agreed that pastors would alternate between denominations and serve terms of six years. The term of service has now been extended to eight years. The three Presbyterian pastors to date have been chosen by a congregational search team. The two Methodist pastors so far have been appointed by their bishop.

A Fast Start

The Brandermill Church was officially born on November 6, 1977, in their restaurant site. One hundred twenty charter members from fifty-two families cast their lots with the new congregation, its covenant, and its newly elected administrative board. A charter document was signed by each new member, including one signature in Chinese by a member who is still actively involved in the church. Most of the new members presented themselves by transfer of membership letters from other churches. Five new Christians professed their faith and requested baptism, four by sprinkling and one by immersion. In the larger charter group were forty-one Presbyterians, thirty-three Methodists, thirteen Episcopalians, eight Baptists, six Congregationalists, and a rich mixture of other denominational families. It was a truly ecumenical beginning for a distinctly community-based church. Its official name reflects its sense of special mission, The Brandermill Church.

Brandermill's members had a clear choice and chose for the long term. The decision to join a church largely revolves around two questions. The "magnet" question is, "What brought you here to this church?" The "glue" question is, "What has kept you in this church?" Brandermill enjoys a highly unusual characteristic. Twenty-eight, or 23 percent, of its charter members are still actively involved in the congregation after thirty years. In our highly mobile contemporary society, a percentage above one in five is a miracle.

On January 22, 1978, Presbyterian D. Clyde Bartges was formally installed as the founding pastor. Clyde had experience as organizing minister for another new church plant in Florida, had helped Presbyterians in Florida select and purchase sites for new congregational starts, and had served as first minister at the nearby Salisbury Presbyterian Church. His background served him well in his leadership of the church during its defining and formative years. Clyde also had the gift of recruiting men and entire families for Brandermill.[8]

During The Brandermill Church's first Christmas season, the fellowship observed a special candlelight worship service under the stars with more than two hundred members and guests in attendance. Early growth in Sunday morning participation and activities forced a necessary move from temporary facilities in Sunday Park to Clover Hill High School. As growth continued, a permanent building was soon needed and planned. Two property parcels were purchased in Sunday Park for $97,500. Each denomination contributed half of the purchase costs. An open sanctuary overlooking the lake was designed, bonds were sold, ground was broken on August 5, 1979, and the first worship service was held on October 19, 1980. For worship services, a hymnal was chosen that had not been published by either sponsoring denomination. When Clyde Bartges retired from fulltime ministry in 1982, Brandermill Church had received 500 believers into its membership during his pastorate, with roughly half from each of the major sponsoring denominations. The church was establishing itself as a flexible perennial community of faith in the Sunday Park section of Brandermill.

Together in Service

As an exercise in self-definition, some new congregations choose to build high fences around their ministry practices, their theological positions, or their modes of governance. They interpret themselves narrowly and zero in on slender ministry niches. Churches of this style and demeanor are referred to by sociologists as "bounded" groups. In contrast, The Brandermill Church chose to be a "centered" church and set its sails in other directions:

- It affirmed its identity as an ecumenical congregation.
- It found middle ground for the administration of its sacraments.
- It chose a worship hymnal with links to neither sponsoring denomination.
- It blended its governance style with features from both sponsoring denominations.
- It alternated its pastoral selection between the two denominations.
- It contributes a tithe of 10 percent of its members' gifts to benevolence causes beyond the local congregation, with 60 percent of this tithe shared equally between the sponsoring judicatories.
- It declared, most importantly, its basic purpose:

We the members of Brandermill Church, recognizing that "there is one body and one Spirit...one Lord, one faith, one baptism, one

God and Father of us all, who is above all and through all and in all," and further recognizing and affirming the evangelical and reformed historical roots of our two sponsoring denominations, do hereby commit ourselves to be an ecumenical congregation in the Brandermill community, witnessing through all aspects of the Church's life to our unity in Christ.[9]

The new communion described itself as a community church, a church in a defined community being the church for that entire community. Ecumenical means, literally, a habitation for the universe, so an ecumenical church pitches a big tent over its part of the world. The Brandermill Church's breadth or ecumenicity is its focus, its distinctive characteristic, and its strength.

Keeping Differences from Becoming Divisions

Differences and diversity can enrich a faith community or divide it. Breadth, flexibility, and freedom are precious characteristics of community churches. They are also messy qualities, creating paradoxes and difficult dilemmas. Leaders of union churches are faced with keeping potential anxiety and frustration at healthy and functional levels.

The Early Church as recorded in Acts offers a stark example of a healthily growing but diverse faith community. New believers from an array of world religions, ethnicities, and languages populated the emerging churches beyond Jerusalem. In the thirty years or so covered by the book of Acts, the Gospel swept across the known world. While keeping the kingdom of God as its central quest, the Church bridged cultures without being derailed by tension, conflict, and unrest. The Holy Spirit, mentioned more than forty times in the first ten chapters alone, helped the new believers transcend the natural differences in their communities.

Life has many potential built-in paradoxes. Some common polarities naturally tug at the hearts of churches:

- stability in tension with change
- local needs in tension with global hurts
- individual interests in tension with team functions
- members' home and personal demands in tension with congregational needs
- tradition in tension with new ideas
- diversity in tension with uniformity
- inclusiveness in tension with exclusivity

Union churches have all of these tensions—and more. Their special hybrid pedigree of differing denominational ties creates unique blends of polarities and problems.

Living between Polarities

Congregational behavior flows naturally from congregational beliefs. Denominational churches can find difficulties in sorting out exactly how a new church will understand and define itself. The challenges of union churches are multiplied by diversity itself. Drawing members from varied denominational backgrounds can potentially open the door to lots of "I've always thought that..." conversations or some "I believe that..." debates. Even Brandermill Church's pastors, more fully schooled in the nuances of differing theological perspectives, brought their personal backgrounds, understandings, and convictions to the table; but they avoided doctrinal debates. In fact, some members have observed their pastors going to extra lengths to be fair to the denomination to which they didn't belong.[10] The flexible perennial nature of Brandermill paved the way for creative ministry.

Outsiders and guests of the congregation are naturally curious about the ways diverse issues are dealt with in a union church. How do Methodists and Presbyterians deal together with their distinctively different traditions? How are debating societies avoided and renewal centers developed? How does Brandermill Church live between its polarities of belief and behavior? The founding pastor reports that when he went to Presbyterian meetings, folks would ask him when Brandermill would become a Methodist church. In contrast, Methodists from beyond the church would ask him when Brandermill would become a Presbyterian congregation. Apparently, even the sponsoring groups realized managing polarities is tricky in practice and has no guarantees.

How, for instance, has Brandermill Church managed the classic polarity[11] between Presbyterianism's emphasis on God's sovereignty and predestination and Methodism's stress on God's grace and religion of the heart? The tension between these doctrinal issues predates Calvin and Wesley, but they do create contrasts in thought and practice. What makes these matters true polarities?

- They are ongoing paradoxes.
- They are independent alternatives.

These contrasts both have upsides that can strengthen the community. They push the community to higher purposes if these polarities can be held in creative tension.

A freestanding Presbyterian or Methodist church would have no reason to manage these polarities. In fact, they might very well make their distinctive beliefs even more visible and starkly presented. In contrast, Brandermill welcomes both traditions and has found ways to live under a broad tent. The church, out of necessity, has found the advantages of both-and thinking and has developed practices that handle complexity, capitalize on diversity, and minimize potential conflicts in the community.

How has this polarity been used for long-term effectiveness? Maybe a distinction of community churches is an ongoing conversation between faith traditions and heritages and across unfolding life stages. Let's go back to the polarity between predestination and free will to see how Brandermill has managed that polarity. The church's new member materials explore this polarity.

Bridging the Gaps

God's sovereignty, his absolute control over the universe and his absolute independence from any other power or will, is a primary affirmation of the Presbyterian Church and Calvinism. God's intentionality is explained in his decrees and is active in all human affairs. The Lord God omnipotent reigns. Predestination applies God's sovereignty to his call of us into a special relationship and destiny. In the mystery of God, he chooses us whether we know it or not.

Total depravity means no aspect of humanity has escaped the taint of our sin and selfishness. Worse yet, there's no way, humanly speaking, to reverse our fallen state. Our consciences are too marred to perceive goodness completely. Our wills are too marred to do God's good, even if we knew it. God alone can call us into the Christian life, and only he can guide us in the process of sanctification within the limitations of this imperfect life.

On the other hand, Methodists affirm that none of us is excluded from the operation of God's powerful grace. Wesley stressed that grace was for all and grace was in all. In fact, grace is active in us in three ways. Prevenient grace claims God is at work from the beginning of our lives, coaxing us toward salvation. God's image is never completely erased from any of us, regardless of the depths of our rebellion. No matter if we know it or not, God is wooing us toward a saving relationship with him. Justifying grace assures believers of an awakening, a new birth, that saves, loves, forgives, and elects us for life-change. Sanctifying grace is God's continuing leavening of our lives after our conversions.

Methodists also emphasize hearts strangely warmed by God. Conversion begins our transformation in Christ, offering our lives and passions to God. Our lives take on new directions as faith works in love. Personal faithfulness yields good works. The inner assurance of our relationship to Christ is demonstrated in compassion, justice, and devotion. We don't earn salvation, but we work to keep it. Disciplined, holy living in our faith journey helps us to grow in grace and to progress toward perfection.

How has Brandermill Church actually dealt with the polarities of predestination and free will?[12] By basing its common life on the meeting point of God's grace, the congregation has found a powerful basis for faith and practice. God's providence directs us. God cares for us, guards us, and guides us. We are dependent on his mercy and grace. As the hymn affirms, grace is greater than all our sin. For Brandermill, that's enough. There's no point in debating God's grace. It is enough, more than enough.

Building Flexibly on Polarities

With theological issues at rest, Brandermill Church's pastors have alternated between Presbyterians and Methodists, according to covenant and agreement.[13] Some members describe congregational cycles of growth and stability. Others feel the personality strengths of each of the five pastors account for much of the dynamism of the church's life. Whether called by a congregational search or appointed by a bishop, the congregation has providentially been matched with the right pastors for the next stage of congregational development.

Reverend Steve Bray, the second pastor and the first Methodist, followed founder Clyde Bartges at Brandermill and served from 1982 until 1988. Steve, a Randolph-Macon College and Yale Divinity School graduate, had experience in new member evangelism and in cultivating young adults, backgrounds that served the young, growing congregation well. Since the church had no parsonage, a housing allowance was provided, an unusual situation for Methodist pastors.

A young, energetic church had a young, energetic minister. Growth increased rapidly and steadily. A second worship service was added, making an innovation possible when communion was administered at the rail in the early service and seated in the later worship time. The fellowship hall was completed, and several unique fundraising projects were undertaken. The congregation took responsibility for its financial resources and ministry direction. At one point, the local Methodist churches pushed to start new congregations, and Brandermill entered into a fundraising process for this cause willingly and generously. The first pastor search process was begun a year in advance to insure the transition would go smoothly.

Reverend Tim Roach, the third pastor and the second Presbyterian minister, served Brandermill from July of 1988 to July of 1994. He and the church discovered each other at a "face-to-face" meeting of search teams and prospective pastors. This coordinated conversation sparked mutual interest, and then an on-site visit completed the match. Tim considered serving a union church a privilege and loved the breadth of an ecumenical congregation.

The continuing expansion of the young congregation was exciting. A full-time Christian educator was added to the staff, allowing the children's ministries and family ministries to grow. Connelly Gamble became the first minister of visitation, cultivated prospective members successfully, and remains a participant in the congregation at present. The growing congregation was straining the limits of its facility once again. A study group developed drawings for an expanded building. At the same time, the church reached a new reality—its older members had begun to die. A memorial garden was created to symbolize this new chapter in community life. As Tim neared the end of his service at Brandermill, he encouraged the congregation to extend its pastoral term to eight years for future pastorates, feeling many ministries hit their stride in the fifth year.

Reverend Reggie Tuck, the fourth pastor and the second Methodist minister, came to Brandermill in 1994 and served until 2002. He was the first pastor to fulfill an eight-year term. Reggie was approached by his district superintendent about the vacancy at Brandermill. His strong interest in ecumenical ministries, his marriage to a Presbyterian clergyperson, and his studies at Princeton, a Presbyterian seminary, made him an ideal candidate.

During Reggie's ministry at Brandermill, the church grew and international missions to Haiti and Guatemala were initiated. Extended mission trips moved members beyond their comfort zones and allowed them to experience missions firsthand. The most obvious advance during Reggie's pastorate was the design and construction of a new $3.8 million dollar worship center. Raising funds to pay off the larger facility and empowering the Church Council to lead the congregation were major processes in the life of the church during this era. Reggie led as a strong shepherd, and grief was generated when he completed his term of service and moved on to Blacksburg.

Reverend Gordon Mapes, the current pastor, is the fifth minister overall and the third Presbyterian to serve at Brandermill, arriving on August 1, 2002. Gordon, a native Californian and a graduate of Princeton, understood the Central Virginia culture, having served other churches in Virginia, including the nearby Salisbury Presbyterian Church. He was drawn to the congregation by its ecumenical nature and the challenges of its size and complexity.

Gordon has concentrated on building stronger staff and lay leader teams, helping the congregation look at its ministry opportunities beyond the completion of the large sanctuary, and responding to the needs of persons after the Katrina disaster. Future challenges for Brandermill Church include more depth in spiritual formation, greater breadth in the stewardship of time, talent, and treasure, and more extensions of mission involvement. The future is bright.

Some events galvanize communities. In late February of 2006, two neighborhood teens tragically drown in Swift Creek Reservoir. The community rallied to the week-long search and rescue effort to find the boys and to support their families and friends. On the final Sunday of the search process, Gordon moved in front of the big window overlooking the lake for the morning sermon. He reminded the members of their ministry beyond the church's walls. The dramatic fact that a sad search was then concluding out on the lake punctuated the preached word that morning and sensitized the congregants to the cohesive community in which they lived and served. It also pointed them toward the wider world.

Faith-in-Community Partnerships

Brandermill's community ministry style is reflected in its commitments to mission projects in the community and with other religious groups. The congregation, in partnership with four inner-city Richmond Presbyterian churches, has done several Habitat for Humanity building projects, including raising $40,000 and building in the Merriwood "Habitat subdivision" off South Richmond's Jeff Davis Highway. Brandermill also works with Caritas, a Richmond-area ministry to homeless persons, hosts the Brandermill Community Band, and continues its Scout programs. Yet that's only the beginning of Brandermill's life-changing projects and partnerships.

Making Lives Better One Vitamin at a Time

In cooperation with Fairfield Christian Church, Brandermill, until the country became politically unstable and dangerous for outsiders, did medical mission projects with Haitian Outreach Ministries. The outreach to Haiti began when a physician with background in mission work in Haiti, Eric English, joined Brandermill. At Brandermill, he collected items to be taken to Haiti for distribution. Then, he asked if some members were interested in going to Haiti themselves. In 1997, ten members of Brandermill Church went to Haiti to operate a walk-in medical clinic for a week.[14] That beginning launched a seven-year run of outreach, until political unrest in Haiti caused the trips to be interrupted.

The free medical care was focused on Cite Soleil, "city of the sun," a four-mile-by-four-mile slum with 400,000 inhabitants. Basic needs— diagnosis and treatment of a variety of ailments, eyeglasses, fluoride treatments for children's teeth, and immunizations—were met. In all cases, vitamins were given to enhance the health struggles of these impoverished people. A team of doctors and nurses, plus a dentist and hygienist, provide the needed care. With an improving political climate, Brandermill may soon be invited to resume their outreach to Haiti.

Caring for Creation amid County Challenges

The care of God's creation was the first expectation on humankind, according to Scripture (Gen. 2:15). That expectation remains timely for us as well. Consequently, when Pastor Gordon Mapes sent Tom Pakurar to a national conference on restoring God's creation, held at Lake George, New York, a series of ripples cascaded out from that first pebble in the pond.[15] Five issues were explored at this Presbyterian gathering—loss of agricultural topsoil, threats to water quality, protection of wild places and wild animals, proximity of toxic waste sites to marginalized populations, and the increasing vulnerability of our globe's air and climate resources. Tom and others offered a Sunday school class based on the Lake George conference and a 1990 paper on Restoring the Creation for Ecology and Justice from Presbyterian sources. Expert speakers, including Virginia's Secretary of Natural Resources, supplemented the study materials and challenged the group on themes of water quality, community planning and environmental issues, and electrical power and environmental management. In June of 2006, Caring for Creation became an official ministry of the church.

Members of Brandermill raised the matter of how to apply these concerns for creation to daily living and how to elevate this theme for the good of the church and community. They found both the Presbyterian and Methodist denominations are rich in approaches to stewardship of nature. Using those and other resources, at least two practical examples of the stewardship and the impact of Caring for Creation's partnerships have been evident.

Some members of the church were already involved in "Hands across the Lake," a grassroots community group made up of residents of Brandermill and its sister development on the other side of the lake, Woodlake. The mission of this community group is to protect Swift Creek Reservoir and its water supply. They took the approach that people don't inherit the earth from their ancestors but borrow it from their grandchildren.[16] Hands across the Lake's influence increased when it hired an independent consultant to evaluate the environmental impact of a lakeside development of more than four thousand new homes and, as a result, influenced the plans for the development.

When two teenaged boys drowned in a canoe accident in February of 2006, the church responded immediately to the rescue efforts and with family support. As a preventive response to the tragedy, the congregation sponsored a water safety program in its sanctuary on April 19, 2006, with the county's Parks and Recreation adventure programmer teaching participants of all ages how to deal with cold-water accidents and other boating crises.

Waldo Beach, the Methodist ethicist, took a simple approach to Christian stewardship.[17] He claimed we are to respond to God as Creator and Redeemer by using things, loving persons, and worshiping God.

Beach said the moment-to-moment challenge was never to mix the verb forms and the objects. That's the kind of crisp simplicity that Brandermill's Caring for Creation ministry features.

Surgical Miracles with the Barnabas Foundation

Good lives become even better when our "deep gladness and the world's deep need meet."[18] That's what happened to Joe Covolo on his first mission trip. In December of 1996, he saw a notice on a church bulletin board about a medical team going to Honduras. A lifelong churchman with Catholic and Methodist backgrounds, the fifty-seven-year-old responded to the need and volunteered to join a group of Mennonites from Pennsylvania on the Honduran trip. That's where he found his deep gladness. Joe had one of life's rare holy moments when he felt "bathed in Christ's blood."[19] For the first time in his life, Joe became a missionary. It was a life-changing experience that has led him back to Honduras over and over again.

In partnership with the Barnabas Foundation, an entity of the Virginia Annual Conference of United Methodists, Joe and others participate in medical miracles. In the mountain clinics of Honduras, skilled surgeons, nurses, and willing helpers repair children's cleft palates and cleft lips, defective hearts, water on the brain and other neurological infirmities as well as spina bifida. Such sophisticated medical services are rare among the bottom third of the population of any Third World country.

Rotating teams return nearly every month to heal more brokenness. The advantages and discoveries in regular returns are numerous:

- Specific diagnoses and referrals can be accommodated with planning.
- Medical specialties can often be recruited for particular cases.
- Opportunities for Honduran physicians to observe and assist provide valuable training.
- New volunteers join the rotations and are themselves "bathed in the blood" of Christian service.

A personal spillover discovery for Joe has been finding "what he wants to be when he grows up," a do-it-yourself Christian missionary. He now understands what Jesus meant when he described himself among the least of the world's people, sick, but looked after with compassion (Mt. 25:36). The caregivers of this New Testament story were invited into the presence of Christ and found deep gladness.

Warming the World with Food and Blankets through Church World Service

Since 1996, Brandermill Church, led by Lorraine Weatherford, has raised monies for the "Tools and Blankets" program of Church World Service, the relief, development, and refugee arm of the National Council of Churches.[20] In this endeavor, Brandermill joins hands with thirty-five denominations and a variety of indigenous groups in more than eighty countries around the world. Brandermill's particular interest and success has been in the blanket program. Five dollars buys a sturdy blanket for use as a bed cover, tent, coat, or carrier of belongings. Brandermill, with enthusiastic assistance of the church's children, has raised as much as $7,000 in a single drive and regularly provides $5,000, making the congregation one of the largest contributors in the United States. The blankets are distributed primarily in Third World countries, especially in places where human need has been heightened by natural disasters or wars.

Also in cooperation with Church World Service, Brandermill sponsors Chesterfield County's CROP Walk. This annual fun and fundraising event helps ease world hunger. The church hosts the event for the county, and the walk is mapped out on the paved walks through the Brandermill community neighborhoods and along the lake.

Protecting People through Stove Building in Guatemala

Since 1996 Brandermill has cooperated with the Highland Support Project.[21] The traditional home in Mayan culture used a central fire pit for cooking and heating. These fire pits were unvented, leaving the Mayan families breathing polluted air. Some respiratory experts estimate that living in this smoky atmosphere is the equivalent of smoking three packs of cigarettes each day. The pollution results in chronic lung disease, eye infections, and shortened life spans.

The nonprofit Highland Support Project began its early mission work with home building. Soon, however, the medical problems overpowered the needs for homes—unless they were fitted with vented stoves. The new stoves are made of cement blocks and are roughly 4 ½ feet long, 3 feet wide, and 2 feet high. The block framework is filled 2/3 deep with sand, lined with firebricks, and topped with a metal cook surface. These front-fed woodstoves are airtight and vented by stove pipes through the roofs. The stoves serve as sources for heating and cooking.

Kit Carson has been active in stove building. As he describes it, the stove building process involves advance planning to find families ready for stoves, to enlist area workers willing to mix mortar, and to get materials in place. Then, work teams of ten persons divide into pairs and build three stoves each week for a total of fifteen stoves per trip. Volunteers learn their stove building craft on-site. Families help construct their own stoves, contributing sweat equity.

Several additional projects flow from stove building efforts. Trees are planted in the Guatemalan highlands to replace clear-cut forests. In Richmond's Carytown area, a shop called AlterNatives sells artifacts and jewelry from Central America and Mayan sources. Monies from sales are plowed back into the Guatemalan economy through the Highland Support Project.

What blessings have flowed from Brandermill's stove building efforts?

- Quality of life and health are improved by the stoves.
- Hope is raised as practical care is provided and relationships are formed.
- The faith of volunteers grows, and vocations are changed toward a mission lifestyle.

The stove building project was Brandermill's first international mission team.

Responding to Katrina's Devastation

In partnership with the Presbytery of Mississippi and Presbyterian Disaster Association, Brandermill has, to date, sent five recovery teams to Gulfport, Mississippi, to help rebuild the coastal region after Hurricane Katrina. Early work revolved around replacing roofs and mudding out homes. Current work has shifted to interior repair and restoring electrical and plumbing systems. This recovery process is long-term. Faith-based organizations from all over the United States are providing the most effective post-Katrina recovery ministries.

Leading Flexible Perennials

Flexible perennials launch their life from multiple sources. Consequently, they give extra time and attention to deepening their common life together. They also take a wide-angle view of their backgrounds and foregrounds. Flexible perennial congregations require both-and thinking and leadership:

- Partnering with civic and religious groups is a hallmark of community churches. It's a timely and needed involvement. Participation in a variety of conventional voluntary associations has declined by 25 to 50 percent over the past twenty or thirty years.[22] Flexible perennials create partnerships across boundaries and take ministry into arenas wherever they and their allies have opportunity to work together.[23] Interdependency is a necessity for future success.
- Flexible perennial churches deal creatively with their natural polarities. When a church begins life and ministry with a blended faith family ministry style, it finds ways to incorporate diversity and paradox into its life. To ignore the built-in differences puts the congregation in peril. The good news is that polarity management[24] is a recently refined leadership approach. Leaders are learning to pay less attention to the party line and to listen more carefully to the peripheries of their communities for ideas that are shaping today's realities.
- Flexible perennial churches find "taking turns" and "playing fair"[25] works. One of life's earliest lessons is simply to take turns.

Brandermill's pattern of alternating pastoral leadership between the two sponsoring denominations is an obvious way to share leadership by taking turns. However, the actual practice is not just "being Presbyterian" for a time and then "being Methodist" for a while. The interaction enriches all when both are valued, used, and appreciated. Community churches excel at fostering inclusion. When shaping their futures, they expand the definition of what matters, who matters, and whose voices count.[26]

- Flexible perennial churches maximize their "stickiness." Brandermill creates strong long-lasting ties. The congregation is unusual in the number of charter members who are still actively involved in its life and leadership after thirty years. People remember and remain hungry for meaningful experiences. Building on its uniqueness as a spiritual anchor both for church members and for community residents, the congregation has found effective ways—directly and indirectly—to find, welcome, and involve people in the life of the church.[27] Brandermill has created experiences of worship, fellowship, education, and mission that have made the congregation "sticky" and easy to adhere to over time.[28] When members weep when they describe mission projects' impacts on them and when members can cite the details of complex ministries from memory, it's obvious they've been shaped by their Brandermill experiences.

- Flexible perennial congregations learn, perhaps better and faster than typical denominational churches, that not every "issue" is an issue. A difference doesn't have to foster a debate or a disagreement. Leaders in flexible churches quickly discover how to choose hills worth dying on and how to release minor issues. Having a clear identity doesn't mean defending that uniqueness when no one is questioning it.

- Flexible perennial churches use their multiple beginnings to enrich their presents and futures. The variety of seeds or plantings or bulbs that begin life for perennials is also a mark of community churches. Perhaps having more ways to generate life originally lends more sources of strength in later life. Brandermill's rich array of mission partnerships reflects its rich beginning.

Next Season

Perennial plants always have a "next season." Their flexibility virtually guarantees interesting tomorrows. The same is true for flexible perennial congregations. Brandermill, at thirty, is a mature church, a regional congregation, an active mission-oriented congregation, and a church with a strong future. What will it become in its next season?

PART III

Harvesting Perennial Communities

*Reaping Yields
Today and Tomorrow*

7

Leading Productive Perennials

St. Mark's Church, Burlington, N.C.

Planted by Producers

What's a better signal of future success for a productive perennial congregation than to be planted by producers?[1] In 1885, the founding fathers of St. Mark's Reformed Church were productive farmers, with root systems in German-speaking Reformed Christianity. Being productive themselves, these founding farmers expected things to grow on their farms and at their church.

Productive perennials not only reproduce season after season, they thrive within seasons as well. Well-planned perennial gardens are vigorous three-season growers. They blend plants that are blooming with those that are just beginning to bud and those that have already blossomed and are now providing background texture and beauty. Productive perennial congregations, like St. Mark's, add to their community settings through an array of all-season ministries.

Traditions and Transitions

St. Mark's forebears brought rich backgrounds to North Carolina. German immigrants, many of whom migrated southward from Pennsylvania's Lancaster area in the mid-1740s to find better growing climates in the Piedmont area of North Carolina, bought 25,000 acres of land between the Haw and Deep Rivers from the Lord's Proprietors. They hoped to establish a permanent German colony in the Old North State. That community, they hoped, would cultivate their faith traditions as well as their crops. Most of these farmers had Reformed and Lutheran backgrounds, extending the lineage of the Protestant Reformation in Europe two hundred years earlier. In particular, the strain of believers who would become St. Mark's Church followed the legacy of Ulrich Zwingli, the Swiss reformer. Zwingli had been a priest who had broken with the Roman Catholic Church. He met with Martin Luther, and although they agreed on most issues, they differed on Zwingli's symbolic interpretation of the Lord's Supper and moved in different directions. In practical terms, however, many of North Carolina's Reformed and Lutheran churches maintained close fraternal ties in the colonial and Civil War eras. Even now with two distinct faith traditions, the Reformed and Lutheran churches in North Carolina are frequently located near each other.

The Reformed pattern for congregations rooted itself in North Carolina soil quickly. Churches were begun, Sunday Schools were started, and issue of language in the worship services was confronted. During the early-to-mid 1880s, the language spoken in worship changed from German to English in the churches of the Guilford Charge. It wasn't an easy change, and some of the Reformed brethren dropped out of their churches. But, overall, the transition from German to the English language proved to be of significant value to the Reformed congregations as they reached out to neighbors without German cultural backgrounds.

Beginning Challenges

When St. Mark's was founded in January of 1855, it had thirty-one charter members. The church established itself independently, moving away from the Lutheran side of its European heritage. The name, "St. Mark's," was chosen to honor the earliest gospel to be written in the New Testament. The members chose a fresh location in the Elon area near Boone Station, a stagecoach stop only a quarter of a mile away from the present church site. The little congregation shared a pastor with two other fellowships in the early days. For several years, the members worshiped under a brush arbor during warm weather and then in members' home during the colder months. In 1862, 4.4 acres of timbered land were purchased for $22, and the property was specifically hallowed for a German Reformed church meeting house. The first church building, a white frame structure measuring 40 feet by 60 feet, completed and dedicated in 1863, served St. Mark's for many years.

The church's early years were in a trying time in America's history— the Civil War. Almost all the able-bodied men from the community were in the military, and resources were tight. The oldest tombstone in St. Mark's Cemetery marks the grave of a young Confederate lieutenant, seventeen-year-old William S. May, who died from war wounds in a Wilmington, N.C., hospital on October 12, 1864. One of the early pastors, David Lefever, serving the church from 1889–1891, was a Civil War combatant, having lost an arm in the battle of Spotsylvania Courthouse near Fredericksburg, Va.

The next pastor, James David Andrew, who led the congregation from 1893–1913 as the church emerged from the scars of war, distinguished himself, becoming the president of Catawba College when he left St. Mark's. The college, the sixth oldest college in North Carolina, was begun in 1851 by Reformed leaders to train their next generation of pastors and emerging leaders. History is important to St. Mark's. To this day, St. Mark's buildings preserve the original pulpit, pastor's chairs, Book of Worship, communion table, and communion set. Reformation Hall, a prominent part of current church facilities, reminds today's congregation at St. Mark's of its historic roots in European Christianity. By the twentieth century, the church had established an important religious niche in Burlington's region and beyond.

Connections and Communities

St. Mark's has been aligned with a variety of faith groupings during its history. First, the Reformed church differentiated itself from the Lutheran stream of religious practice in the Piedmont region. Then, in 1934, St. Mark's became an Evangelical and Reformed Church when the two larger bodies merged and selected a new name. In 1957, the United Church of Christ denomination was formed out of a series of unions involving four older faith families—the Evangelical and Reformed, already previously united, and the Congregational and Christian Churches, also previously united. St. Mark's joined the new denomination. Over the next several years, however, St. Mark's grew increasingly uncomfortable and frustrated with some emphases of the national denomination. Letters of concern got responses from the national structures that seemed casual. Rather than withholding or designating funds to specific national ministries, on September 16, 1973, St. Mark's became the first church to withdraw from the Southern Conference of the United Church of Christ. When St. Mark's couldn't in good conscience enthusiastically and energetically support the direction of the larger body, the congregation decided to be faithful to the Gospel in its own way.

Another change happened locally. Since the early days of the twenty-first century, the "Reformed" descriptor has been laid aside, and the church now sees itself as an interdenominational fellowship. Seekers without a religious background were confused. They wondered what bad things the church had done that required it to "reform" itself.

Rather than explaining endlessly, the church decided simply to drop the Reformed terminology. In the congregation's guest information booklet, St. Mark's positions itself as an interdenominational church made up of people from a wide variety of Christian backgrounds, and not connected to a particular denomination.[2] The beliefs, values, and practices of St. Mark's remain as always, however, firmly rooted in the deep currents of New Testament belief and practice.

A Perennial Church Faces Faith's Perennial Question

On April 16, 1978, Robert Milton Disher Jr. was installed as the fourteenth and current pastor of the church. Bob's ministry has involved a variety of changes that have created the current congregation's style and atmosphere. Under Bob's leadership, growth was not the central issue. The question that eventually haunted Bob later was a deeply theological issue: Can and will St. Mark's Church be able to reach the population of North Carolina's Piedmont region for the kingdom of God?

Bob's arrival in 1978 at St. Mark's was almost "an arranged marriage." The pastor of Bob's family's United Church of Christ congregation in Lexington, N.C. was a brother of Lawrence A. Leonard, St. Mark's pastor from 1960–1978. Pastor Leonard knew Bob's parents, had watched Bob grow up, and invited Bob to preach an evening series of messages during his final semester at Duke Divinity School. When Bob arrived to preach his series, the veteran pastor told him he'd just announced his retirement from pastoral ministry that very morning. Unknown to Bob, an informal succession plan was underway, and he was auditioning with the congregation. The process took shape quickly. Bob was called shortly as the church's pastor, its youngest pastor at age twenty-five.

St. Mark's was then a traditional church in a changing region. In 1978, the Burlington area was beginning to grow and change its economic focus. Historically part of "The Mill," a textile region stretching in a crescent across North Carolina's Piedmont from Mebane to Gastonia, Burlington was diversifying its economic and manufacturing base. It was a good time for a new cycle of productive ministry for the 150 or so members of St. Mark's who welcomed Bob.

Fresh from seminary with all the energy and enthusiasm of youth, Bob poured himself into the church. Growth followed. In 1982, two wings were added to the original building. By 1988, the church had grown to 500 members, and a second worship service was begun. Space for education and activities were also added. Children's ministries were successful and appreciated. Obviously, the congregation was expanding. But, was God's kingdom growing as well? St. Mark's was showing signs of being a productive perennial congregation, but a perennial question was beginning to echo in Bob's quiet moments. After ten years of successful ministry, the question created holy unrest and ferment in his spirit.

Seeds for New Directions

When a leader has been in a faith community for a decade or more, he or she often becomes a bit out of focus, blinded and deafened to needs beyond that community. It's telling, but not surprising, that the two "prophets" who spoke to Bob's inner self were not part of St. Mark's life. They were outsiders who could and did embody contrasts more powerfully than insiders might be capable of doing.

Revealing encounters with two friends forced Bob to wonder about St. Mark's ability and effectiveness in reaching out to them and to people like them. Friend "A" was an acquaintance from the YMCA. He was radically lost and facing an eternity without Christ. Bob wondered if Friend A became a Christian and joined St. Mark's, would he be able to "speak the language" and be able to understand his faith pilgrimage? Friend "B" was a high school buddy who had moved to Burlington to work. At Bob's invitation, he reluctantly attended a worship service at St. Mark's. He admitted the experience left him in "a time warp." Neither the message nor the music was in his Baby Boomer vernacular. It was a sobering moment when Bob realized the growing church he'd given ten years to as pastor did not easily communicate the Gospel to his nonchurched neighbors. A perennial question for church leaders is: how do we reach our generation for Christ? Bob wasn't sure his former answers would be sufficient for St. Mark's future. It was time to look for better and more productive ministry options. It was time to find and use an "everyday theology."[3]

In 1989, Bob attended a "Leadership 2000" conference in Dallas. Among others, Bill Hybels and John Maxwell spoke. The idea of a missional "Acts 2" church was presented and took root in Bob's imagination. Bob felt called to attempt the Acts 2 model. But he didn't see a way to move forward immediately or confidently. His vision didn't easily become specific or selective. Bob didn't trust his own sense of direction. He did the only thing he knew to do. He waited.

The seeds of a new direction had been planted and were beginning to germinate. For the next three years, Bob fed his ferment by attending conferences at Saddleback Church in Southern California and at Willow Creek Church in suburban Chicago. By the end of a Willow Creek event, Bob had listed seventy-six ministry ideas and actions on a legal pad. Yet the list was just random ideas, not a coherent vision. Those ideas weren't whole or ripe yet. There was nothing to say clearly and forcefully yet. This vision wasn't ready for harvest yet.

One Petal at a Time

Vision is a common theme in pastoral leadership. Some church members seem to assume God speaks only to isolated leaders who come down from their mountains of revelation with a direct and immediate word from on high. They act like God only speaks to one person per congregation and mostly on the leader's schedule. As a consequence, pastoral vision may be disconnected from central congregational needs or from the hurts of the region or even the will of God. Frequently, "instant" visions are nine parts previous practices and old biases and only one part fresh faith. In truth, the growth of vision in congregations is more likely to be a slow process, and authentic vision is always on God's schedule.

Vision speaks for God's futures, matches the needs and resources of the congregation and its context, and stretches the congregation's leadership team. God's futures can't be seen by people who don't have eyes to see, or heard by believers who have unhearing ears (Mt. 13:15). Faithful eyes and ears begin to function finally. Ideas become clear pictures within the congregation's imaginations and are fleshed out in leaders' minds and ministries.

It takes time for visionary ideas to germinate and grow into ministry. One type of tropical bamboo grows unseen underground for three years before it bursts through the surface of the earth and shoots up to ninety feet of height in a single growing season. Sturdy roots are a characteristic of healthy perennial growth, and that root system takes time to develop. But vision emerges powerfully when it becomes clear and strong.

An anonymous poet has beautifully described the organic unfolding of religious vision and calling in the lives of the faithful. These images seem to reflect Bob's patient discovery of a new direction for St. Mark's:[4]

Life unfolds
a petal at a time
slowly.

The beauty of the process is crippled
when I try to hurry growth.
Life has its inner rhythm
which must be respected.
It cannot be rushed or hurried.

Like daylight stepping out of darkness,
like morning creeping out of night,
life unfolds slowly a petal at a time
like a flower opening to the sun,
slowly.

God's call unfolds
a petal at a time.
Like you and I
becoming followers of Jesus,

disciped into a new way of living
deeply and slowly.
Be patient with life's unfolding petals.
If you hurry the bud it withers.
If you hurry life it limps.
Each unfolding is a teaching
a movement of grace filled with silent pauses
breathtaking beauty
tears and heartaches.

Life unfolds
a petal at a time
deeply and slowly.

May it come to pass!

Finally, Bob's sense of clarity about God's calling for him at St. Mark's crystallized, like a flower that bloomed fully in its season.

Responding and Resisting

Even with a decade and a half of relationships in place, when Bob began talking about an outreach ministry to spiritual seekers, St. Mark's got messy. On the other hand, it may have been that decade and a half of relationships that provided a foundation to weather the storm. The messiness was almost predictable. At first blush, most change is unwelcome in most churches, even when it's framed in biblical or theological terms. Practicing the large-scale ideas of the Great Commission and of reaching lost people spoke to the hearts of some members. Other members saw changes in traditional worship and music forms as a betrayal of trust. The former group was moving toward mission, and the latter group was angry and ready to defend the ramparts. One church leader announced the church wasn't for unchurched people. If those unchurched types wanted to join the church, they should clean up, learn the music, and act like the long-time members.

St. Mark's atmosphere became charged, divided, and ugly. In the late fall of 1994, thirty members left. In an attempt to clear the air, in November of 1994 the Church Board hosted a congregational meeting that drew 350 members together for discussion and debate. It was a contentious gathering, but it also settled the missional church issue and moved St. Mark's to reach out deliberately and consistently to the lost of the region. Reminiscent of the language transition from German to English to reach out more effectively more than a century earlier, St. Mark's refocused itself. When vision takes root finally, a tipping point is reached,[5] and the new focus becomes the center of congregational ministry.

Blooming Again

Beginning in 1995, momentum was again alive and well at St. Mark's. High morale has made a difference in church life. Both attendance and giving have grown at double-digit rates as a pattern in recent years. Another interesting area of growth has been expansion of the pastoral staff. When the church began searching for an associate pastor, it decided to customize the job description to balance Bob's strengths and offset his weaknesses. That decision diversified the staffing philosophy and configuration. Now, St. Mark's has nine pastors, rounding out Bob's role as Senior Pastor and Teacher. Reflecting a microcosm of the region's diversity and representing a variety of denominational backgrounds— United Church of Christ, Free Methodist, Quaker, Assembly of God, United Methodist—as well as the full array of gifts and temperaments, the staff is as productive as the congregation itself.

Choosing Seeds, Reaping Harvests

The pastoral staff and members of St. Mark's focus on five key values of faith and orient their current ministry efforts around these arenas:

- community
- growth
- worship
- service
- outreach

Cultivating these core values, St. Mark's, like all productive perennial congregations, blooms all season long. St. Mark's produces at least four distinctive kinds of ministries. It clusters these ministries around three large-scale events and seasons. Key leaders, both clergy and lay, focus St. Mark's productive efforts simply:

- St. Mark's produces stories of God-changed lives. Those deeply personal stories testify to new and deepening faith. They mark God's movement in lives and challenge observers to invite God to stir their lives as well.
- St. Mark's produces surprises in worship. As God moves in congregational gatherings, unpredictable events occur. For some members who have backgrounds in highly structured worship traditions, worship at St. Mark's is an exciting and energizing experience full of surprises and freshness.
- St. Mark's produces missions that "leak" into its community. Perhaps the church profits from not being limited to denominational missions "programs." Members, rather than being "loyal" to some distant denominational headquarters, live their faith locally and create pervasive involvement in community helping groups.

- St. Mark's produces three anchors for its annual calendar of ministries. Christmas Eve anchors the late fall and early winter. Easter anchors late winter and early spring. The church has discovered a third anchor that serves St. Mark's uniquely. The final Sunday in August features a large-scale baptism celebration at a lake and launches the fall season. St. Mark's, like perennials in general, is a three-season community.

Describing the Yield of the Harvest

St. Mark's affirms twelve principles as guides for its common life and faith. To the congregation's great credit, it lives these values rather than casually tipping its hat to them from time to time:

1. People who are living their lives separated from Christ are important to God and are vitally important to us as a church.
2. Full devotion to Christ is normal for every believer.
3. The Bible is God's word and is relevant to our contemporary culture.
4. God's power for ministry is released through prayer.
5. Genuine worship can be meaningful and relevant both to believers and to those who seek a relationship with God.
6. Every believer should be serving in his or her spiritual gift area.
7. Life change happens best in small groups.
8. Pastors are charged with the responsibility of mobilizing, equipping, and releasing believers for ministry.
9. Excellence honors God, reflects God's character, and inspires people to invest in God's work.
10. St. Mark's Church should continue to grow until every person in Burlington, N.C., and the surrounding communities has heard the Gospel.
11. A healthy church is characterized by people who are redeemed and sent out for ministry.
12. Discipleship is best accomplished one life at a time.

These basic values provide the functional compass for the church, its ministries, and its outreach.

Cultivating Productive Community

St. Mark's Church has a straightforward mission: "To connect people to Christ and to one another." Christians know that Jesus came to seek and save the lost (Lk. 19:10). St. Mark's intends to do the same. St. Mark's reminds us that Jesus did more than rescue people from hell. He also wanted to make them fit for heaven and bring the values of God's Kingdom to Earth. At St. Mark's, people meet Christ and then grow in their faith as they become conformed to his character. Community is one result of salvation, spiritual formation, and service.

The emergence of Christian community at St. Mark's is only one step in fulfilling Christ's mission. They are a gathered church because they are called and redeemed to be together and to represent Christ with their unified diversity. As a biblical community, they then attempt to scatter and extend God's kingdom locally and globally as salt and light.

The membership cultivates Christian community in a variety of ways, particularly in worship and in small groups. St. Mark's hosts a casual, informal Newcomer's Coffee as a get acquainted gathering following each of the weekend worship services. This meet-and-greet allows newcomers to meet staff and leaders and to learn about ways to become involved in the life of the community. St. Mark's also offers a three-week class about membership in the church, without pressuring newcomers to join. Additionally, St. Mark's provides an introduction to their small group model. Anybody who wants to join the St. Mark's family can find a place at the table.

Cultivating Productive Growth

A seat at the table is only the beginning. St. Mark's provides a rich array of spiritual formation avenues. Rather than using a traditional ladder model of climbing upward in the Christian life, St. Mark's provides a merry-go-round of spiritual development. All of St. Mark's participants are invited to get on the merry-go-round of growth at their pace and preference.

Every participant at the church is invited to several basic growth opportunities designed by Eric Allred, leader of Spiritual Development, and his team of volunteers. "Tough Questions" is a discussion forum for skeptics and seekers to wrestle with big issues about God and Christianity. "Starting Point" is a basic study for those who are either beginning or returning to a relationship with Christ. "Foundations" is an overview and application of the essential beliefs of the Christian faith. "DISCIPLE" is an intensive thirty-four–week journey through the Old and New Testaments. Novice Bible students are welcome, and the course intends to position believers in the story of redemption. Additionally, Bible studies for men and women meet at various times and places throughout the week. These and other growth disciplines stimulate seekers and fully devoted followers of Christ to become more like him.

Life change, rather than mere information, is the goal of St. Mark's efforts at spiritual formation. Ruth Bresson, St. Mark's adult ministries' leader, relates to a broad range of audiences, including those in the mentoring events she provides for women, singles, and persons in recovery. The link Ruth and others provide between spiritual formation and Christian service is basic to church life in a missional style.

St. Mark's recognizes the value of volunteers' own health and growth in an unusual way. They "let the ground rest." Using the Old Testament idea of letting land lie fallow for a season of restoration, Cindy Bailey, leader of Children's Ministries, gives her regular teachers and workers the summer off. In contrast with most churches, St. Mark's doesn't "take the teens off the parent's hands" during the summer season. Jarm Turner, leader of Student Ministries, while providing an array of mission trips and summer camps, frees students for more time with their families as well.

Cultivating Productive Worship

Worship at St. Mark's is more than weekend gatherings at the church, as essential as that experience is to believers and seekers. To extend and enrich the worship services themselves, "An Ordinary Day with Jesus," a six-week study to help participants to welcome Christ's presence in every moment of life and to know the close connection to God everyone hopes for, is offered.

Cindy Bailey demonstrates the importance of parents providing weekday faith growth opportunities for their children. Cindy shows parents two bottles of marbles, one with 3000 marbles representing the hours parents have with their children annually and one with forty marbles representing the hours church leaders have with those same children in a year. Even if the church does the quality of ministries to and with children that St. Mark's provides, it's not enough. "Crew Time," an after-worship luncheon for parents and children, furnishes coaching moments for parents as well as a CD that encourages parent-child conversations and devotions to be shared and discussed. This ministry is another part of St. Mark's family-friendly atmosphere.

Steve Flint, leader of Worship Arts, shepherds worship design and planning. Artists with various talents—musical art, dramatic art, visual art, and video art—help lead worship at St. Mark's. As part of their own journeys in the believer's worshiping life, they facilitate knowing God in worship gatherings. These artists reach across the full range of tastes and life backgrounds as they lead contemporary worship. They present life-change stories from the grist of their own lives.

St. Mark's, while a young church overall, has more than 400 members who are 65 and older. When these older members die and are memorialized, they often want their funerals to be held in the original sanctuary, according to Ben Bishop, leader of Pastoral Care. That's the setting where many of their most profound religious experiences occurred. One of the challenges seeker-sensitive congregations face is to find ways to use the Christian faith's symbols and rituals as anchors for life's transitions and belief's deeper stages.

Cultivating Productive Service

St. Mark's challenges its members to discover their spiritual gifts and to leaven their world, beginning in their home region. On one early March weekend in 2007, "INSIDE-OUT" at St. Mark's mobilized members to make a difference in thousands of lives across Alamance County. The congregation hosted a forum that brought together twenty-five benevolent organizations in the county to channel the 500 volunteers in attendance into sixty-two projects. This event was based on a simple belief: no other expression has the power to convey Christ's love and compassion as when we unselfishly serve another person. Simple acts of service can turn the world upside down and inside out. The church became God's hands extended that day and beyond.

Some of the service options are familiar types of mission projects for many churches these days—Habitat for Humanity, Easter Seals, Christian Counseling Center, Meals on Wheels, and hospice. But some projects are tailored specifically to local needs, and St. Mark's members reach out to those persons and helping organizations. Included in these challenges are the following:

- AlaMap provides medications and counseling to healthcare patients.
- Allied Churches meets the emergency needs of persons who are without a place to stay, a place to eat, or other basic requirements.
- Garrett and Smith Elementary Schools benefit from partnering with St. Mark's.
- Alamance Pregnancy Center counsels women with unwanted pregnancies.
- Piedmont Rescue Center serves the community's homeless.
- Family Abuse Services tries to prevent or intervene in situations of domestic violence and child abuse.
- Friendship Adult Services offers alternatives to institutional care by providing social interaction for adults.
- The Kopper Top Life Learning Center offers recreational therapy to disabled individuals to enhance their quality of life.
- Loaves and Fishes is a ministry that provides groceries to persons and families who live on life's margins.
- Ralph Scott Lifeservices helps those living with developmental disabilities toward a better quality of life.
- Residential Treatment Services offers care and assistance for the rehabilitation of adults with mental illness, alcoholism, and drug addiction.
- Twin Lakes, a continuing care retirement community, involves St. Mark's members.
- The VP Foundation sponsors research and treatment for those coping with painful connective tissue disease.

St. Mark's does a remarkable job of weaving its members into the fabric of its local community and making Christian service a foundational and expected feature of living the life of faith.

Cultivating Productive Outreach

St. Mark's reaches out to unchurched, dechurched, and dissatisfied persons. Every member is encouraged in "Becoming a Contagious Christian." A bold outreach effort at St. Mark's is its multi-site ministry in Eastern Alamance County's Mebane community. Launched in September of 2005 and led by Scott Woody, Executive/Multi-Site Pastor, with assistance from Tim Riddle, Executive/Media Pastor, the new site demonstrates St. Mark's blend of nerve and verve.

Research showed 60 percent of Alamance County, N.C., is unchurched, and neighboring Orange County is 70 percent unchurched. Since both counties are expanding rapidly, Mebane was an obvious outreach opportunity. Operating on the assumption that unchurched folks are unlikely to travel more than fifteen miles to church, establishing an additional site of St. Mark's was a logical step. The advantages of multi-site ministry were also obvious: a small church atmosphere with big church resources, increased convenience, and greater accessibility. Bob teaches via video at the Mebane site, while Scott serves as site pastor. Progress and growth have been good to date.

Leading Productive Perennial Congregations

Like the founding farmers who planted St. Mark's, just existing or merely living isn't an option. Growth is expected. Three-season production is central. What's distinctive about leaders in productive perennial churches? What do these leaders do to remain productive?

Productive leaders never forget the harvest.

Productive leaders think about reproductive ministry. Like the basic management question, they ask, "What business are we in? What result do we intend?"[6]

They understand that harvests involve lots of hands—believers who plant, cultivate, water, wait, and ultimately put the harvest squarely in the redemptive hands of God (1 Cor. 3:6). St. Mark's uses the two most visible Christian holiday seasons, Christmas and Easter, as occasions to cultivate and nurture persons toward relationships with Christ. These seasons invite persons into the fellowship of the church and its spheres of influence. Then, their third "high holy day," their baptism celebration on a lake in August, provides a tangible culmination of God's harvest. The entire church year points to that harvest day.

Productive leaders know when to cut their losses.

Productive leaders recognize what Seth Godin calls "the dip,"[7] the sinkhole where the euphoria of starting anew fades into a nonproductive slog. When a ministry or program is no longer worth the outcome or leads to a dead-end or causes you to flounder along, then you may be in the dip and probably should quit making that effort any longer. In the early 1990s, Bob saw the waning of St. Mark's effectiveness in reaching people new to Burlington. After a careful search he finally found a way to stop that trend and reach out powerfully.

Just quoting Vince Lombardi's dictum, "Quitters never win, and winners never quit," is not enough. In truth, real leaders quit all the time. In fact, that distinguishes them from non-leaders. They are discerning of God's emerging directions. They quit when "the right things at the right time" are clearly no longer right for them. Quit the wrong things. Stick with the right things. Pray for a clear head and heart to discriminate the one from the other.

Productive leaders are growers.

The German farmers who established St. Mark's knew one life truth from their experience in agriculture: you're always only one bad crop year away from disaster. The same applies to today's churches. A major ministry failure—a program that bombs, a minister who falls, or a conflict that divides—can doom a congregation. Consequently, productive leaders are perpetual growers—growth in themselves and in others. They never take their eyes off the prize—God's harvest. They grow the kingdom of God by helping people be formed in and conformed to Christ. So foundational is the organic concept of Christian harvest that "a harvest mentality must be central to everything we do."[8]

Productive leaders are other-oriented.

Shorter-term leaders, like annual plants, often tend to be more self-focused. They too frequently reflect the old prayer:

Bless me and my wife,
My son, John, and his wife,
We four,
No more.

Happily, that sentiment isn't the routine intention of perennial leaders who think longer-term, particularly about others and how to reach them. St. Mark's is a "seeker-sensitive" church. That commitment shows up in several ways, including aggressive evangelism and social outreach from those who "have food to spare" to those who have an array of human and spiritual needs (Lk. 15:17).

Productive leaders multiply ministries.

Perennials grow across time and amid other plants. While annuals prefer monocultures and like to grow with their own kinds of plants, perennials enjoy polycultures and prefer "mixed meadows." Their example guides productive leaders.

Productive leaders are experimental and entrepreneurial.

They think in multiples. They peer over more than one horizon at a time. Look at St. Mark's. The congregation is "multiple" in lots of ways—sites, generations, those who are seeking God and those who have found Christ, levels of commitment, stages of faith, faith formation approaches, surprises in worship, and appealing to the "in's," "out's," and "back-again's." St. Mark's risks sowing lots of seeds in lots of seedbeds to reach as many different persons as possible.

Produce, Produce, Produce

Productive perennial congregations remind us that the Gospel is literally "down to earth." In fact, the first task God gave Adam, Eve and their descendents was to plant and tend gardens. The challenge hasn't changed fundamentally since the Creation. We Christians are called to plant, cultivate, and harvest God's increase for his kingdom. We are expected to be perennial producers. We are still the farmers who go out to sow (Mk. 4:3). We exercise faith when we risk a seed to the soil.

8

Leading Futuristic Perennials

Second Presbyterian Church,
Roanoke, Va.

Naming Tomorrow

Roanoke has always looked for better ways to describe its history and destiny. When the first European explorers visited the Roanoke Valley in the seventeenth century, they traveled the trail between Maryland and Tennessee through the Blue Ridge Mountains. The salt marshes they found in the area gave the village its original name, "Big Lick," after that life-essential resource for humans and animals. Later, in 1884, Roanoke was chartered as a city by the Virginia legislature and renamed for the river that runs through it. "Roanoke" is an Algonquin word for the shell money the tribe used. Maybe being named for currency was prophetic.

During and after America's colonial era, Roanoke emerged as a hub of trails and roads. The Great Wagon Road, one of the fledgling nation's first "superhighways," linked Philadelphia with the Roanoke Gap. At the Roanoke Gap, the Great Wagon Road divided, taking some settlers south to Carolina's Piedmont and delivering others along the Wilderness Road southwest to Tennessee and Kentucky.

After the Civil War, Roanoke quickly became a transportation town. The little city boomed when it became a rail connector for the transportation of coal from the Pocahontas fields of Southwestern Virginia and West Virginia north to Columbus and Cincinnati, Ohio, and south to Durham and Winston-Salem, North Carolina. When mergers created the Norfolk and Western Railway, Roanoke was chosen as the new railroad's headquarters. Roanoke wholeheartedly took to the romance of being a railroad town. The city grew almost magically. As the twentieth century dawned, it became known informally as "Magic City."

Manufacturing boosted Roanoke's economy as well. The Norfolk and Western's Roanoke Shops built steam locomotives for most North American railroads as long as that market lasted. Textiles arrived when American Viscose opened its rayon production operation in 1917. Although both the rail center and the rayon plant and many of their employees are now gone, Roanoke still ships goods and services to the United States via Interstate 81 and other cross-country routes.

Roanoke, currently developing a new identity as a medical services and research center, boasts nearly 100,000 souls in the midst of a larger cluster of growing counties. The city is sheltered by the illuminated star on Mill Mountain and is now known as the Star City of the South. The town, morphing across time from the frontiers of salt to rail to manufacturing to medicine, has come a long way and still has a journey ahead.

Faith on the Frontier

In the early days of statehood, many Presbyterians, Episcopalians, and Baptists migrated through the Shenandoah Valley south to Roanoke. They wasted no time establishing churches in the region. In 1851, the Montgomery Presbytery began the Old Lick Presbyterian Church in present downtown Roanoke. The church moved to another inner-city location in 1875 and renamed itself Big Lick Presbyterian Church. When Roanoke was chartered in 1884, the church renamed itself, initially Roanoke Presbyterian Church and later First Presbyterian Church. The city grew fast, and so did the church. Outgrowing its building, First Presbyterian decided to launch another church.

In 1891 the mother church planted the Second Presbyterian Church.[1] The new church was situated high above Roanoke's center on the same block it has now inhabited for more than a century. That orientation toward the city proved to be prophetic. The original address was on Highland Avenue on the side of the property farthest from the central business district. In the 1960s when the church chose to stay in the core city, it changed its address to Mountain Avenue, the street nearest to downtown, so it would "always face the city."[2] During that era when many of America's churches left the inner cities, First Presbyterian Church moved to the suburbs. Consequently, Second Presbyterian has gradually taken on the role of the "Old First Church,"[3] the denominational anchor congregation with characteristic emphases on quality ministries and breadth in the membership.

Second Presbyterian[4] has a sense of destiny, so it has never felt a need to be trendy. In the face of local economic booms and busts as well as amid worldwide wars and the Great Depression, the church has grown reliably in both membership and in resources. Preaching, great music, and formal worship were, and remain, hallmarks for the congregation. The impressive grey stone buildings and parking areas fill the entire block between Mountain and Highland Avenues and between Second and Third Streets, plus two lots and a house across the way. In the early days, Second Presbyterian was a "walk to" church with many members in the Old Southwest neighborhood. Across many years, Second Presbyterian Church has been a reservoir of leadership for the community and beyond. The congregation's members are highly visible on local boards and in the leadership of service groups, contributing over time two governors for the Commonwealth of Virginia.

Rooted in Roanoke

The stability and strength of the congregation across its one hundred plus years are noteworthy. Only four pastors—H. Spencer Edmunds, A. Hayden Hollingsworth, Jr., William R. Klein, and George C. Anderson—have served the church since 1923. The tongue-in-cheek comment around Second is that pastors arrive when they're thirty-eight and stay twenty-six years. Literally true in a couple of instances, the pattern of long terms of service is common in the church. Second Presbyterian is a place where pastors and lay leaders choose to associate, contribute, and then stay on and on. Like all leaders, pastors leave their signatures on their churches, particularly if they have extended tenures.

Spencer Edmunds[5] (1923–1941) put a friendly face on Second. During one ten-year period, he made 6000 pastoral calls, mostly to hurting people and prospective members. Spencer was a biblical preacher with down-to-earth messages. In his first sermon at Second, he defined the work of the church "to evangelize the world and to nourish and sustain the lives of those who become Christians."[6] He was a joiner and a golfer, using both to make friends in the community for Second. Many of the new members at Second were among the leaders of the Roanoke community. The church grew in spite of the hardships of the Depression, establishing the Franklin Road Mission, beginning to rotate leaders and officers, and bringing Mary Bigham on staff to lead Christian education and Jeanne Martin Marshall to develop the first volunteer choir.

Hayden Hollingsworth,[7] affectionately called "Doctor Holly," served as Second's pastor from 1942 until 1968. Arriving amid a difficult era of war and neighborhood change, Hollingsworth, a serious personality, was a builder and a practical preacher of applied Christianity. During his first year, he visited all the families of the church in their homes. In the decade after the end of World War II, the church grew from 800 to 1500. Always interested in foreign missions, Hayden served on the national denomination's mission board. With the railroad at its peak, Second Presbyterian built a chapel and an education building, expanded parking areas, opened a preschool, emphasized stewardship, began a businessmen's luncheon, and brought Mrs. K.F. Macy on staff as church hostess. Additionally, memorial windows in stained glass with biblical motifs were installed in the sanctuary.[8] Significantly, after a self-study, Second Presbyterian decided deliberately to remain a downtown congregation.

Bill Klein[9] (1968–1991) came to the pastorate at Second, in part, because the church had chosen to face the challenges of the core city. Upon arrival, the Klein family found three pleasant heritages for the minister at Second, owing largely to the Edmunds and Hollingsworth pastorates: the pastor and his family were permitted to laugh, have problems, and be normal folks; the pastor was expected to be involved with the youth of the church; and the pastor had a voice in the selection of officers. Bill was another in the lineage of powerful preachers, rooting his sermons in the most thoughtful theology of the time and delivering them to a television audience as well as to the gathered church. Second's members both expected great preaching and affirmed it. Bill helped the church reach into the community to heal a myriad of hurts. The first woman elder and the first woman deacon were selected in 1969. The Second Presbyterian Fund, approaching two million dollars now, was founded in 1978. A Girl's Club was begun to reach out to the immediate neighborhood. Looking at the world, mission projects overseas, including Brazil, Honduras, and Costa Rica, were expanded.

George Anderson, the current pastor and only the seventh pastor at Second Presbyterian, began his ministry in Roanoke in 1998. George is forward thinking. Because he is good at keeping his eye on the ball, he is a steward of the long-term health of the church. Treating the congregation as a family, he is gifted at reaching all ages and helps Second strengthen its multi-generational community. George acts strategically, choosing which ministry to invest himself in and then deciding when to act.

George's arrival at Second was an extended, deliberative process. The long interim between Bill Klein's retirement and the beginning of George's ministry involved two interim ministers who served three terms of service. Richard G. Hutcheson, a retired Navy chaplain and admiral, served first and brought all the polish of a gentleman and an officer. Dick was followed for a year by J. Eade Anderson, a retired minister from Montreat, N.C. He was an approachable person with a charming

Mississippi drawl. The hidden element in Eade's term of service was that, when his own son, George, was later called as pastor, the church had already had the opportunity to evaluate and become comfortable with George's personal style. Then, after Eade's departure and before George's arrival, Dick Hutcheson returned for another term of service.

During a time when some churches "take a vacation," Second recruited new members and shouldered responsibility for ministry. While the extended interim period was unusual for Second, it served the practical purpose of showing that Second Presbyterian Church was a deeper and wider congregation than any single pastor or any one ministry style.

Ably serving with George in pastoral ministry were Nancy M. Morris, associate pastor for Christian Education; L. Gerald Carter, Director for Congregational Care; Phil Boggs, church administrator; Jeffrey and Marianne Sandborg in the area of music; and age-group specialists form a gifted leadership team. George is credited with introducing an in-depth biblical survey to Second's members. The DISCIPLE Bible Study program has provided both a deeper perspective on scripture and deeper community for its participants. As mentioned in chapter 7, the program takes thirty-two to thirty-four weeks to grow casual students of the Bible into sturdy Christian disciples.

Another option after DISCIPLE is the Christian Believer course, a disciplined study of foundational beliefs as explored by theologians across all eras of church history. Some members report that DISCIPLE has helped them grow into informed and more serious persons of faith.

Foundations for the Future

Second Presbyterian has grown from generations of solid leadership in the pews and in the pulpit. Stability helps congregations know themselves and feel "solid as rocks." Second is a church that does the basics of faith and fellowship with excellence and reaches a wide spectrum of members from across the Roanoke Valley. Heritage is used as a springboard to tomorrow rather than a place to rest in the past and present. When the church held a celebratory dinner for members with fifty years of tenure, one hundred people attended.

Business leaders tell us that good commercial products rely on quality and consistency. When Henry John Heinz began producing his famous ketchup in 1876, he observed: "To do a common thing, uncommonly well, brings success."[10] Second does the common basics of faith development—worship, education, music, stewardship, family ministries, and missions—uncommonly well with quality and consistency. That's an asset for perennial health.

Second has remained remarkably free from conflicts, factions, and cynicism. It's a place where opinions are shared, not argued, a place graced with good decision-making skills. Trust and shared leadership have been hallmarks of the church. Since Second has no ruling clique, it has remained a church where all its members feel ownership. Perhaps, most importantly, Second Presbyterian, Roanoke, is a congregation that knows who it is and understands how to welcome its future. Second recognizes that its "second century" is unfolding, and it is taking a hundred year view as it positions itself strategically for its life and future.

One of the interesting themes in reviewing Second Presbyterian's Web site, book of history, and member recruiting video is the value the church places on the young. Many church histories make few, if any, references to the minister's family, but *A "Second" Century* provides rich information about ministers' spouses and children. Additionally, church staffers, including interns, and their contributions are discussed with pride and in some detail. The church has a renowned preschool and also makes investments in the future of their young people with scholarships in memory of Hayden Hollingsworth, Ed and Edith Johnson, and Mary Bigham. George Anderson's unique baptisms are high worship experiences for many. Many of the neighborhood outreach programs have also been oriented to the children of Old Southwest and the Roanoke Valley. The view of children and youth is often a clue to how a congregation sees its future.

First Identity, Then Intention

Perennial plants develop across seasons and years. The rhythms of seasons bring their own challenges and give their own rewards. Perennials pace themselves as they move toward the future. They rotate times of high energy with times of respite. Above all, perennials constantly look ahead. They enrich their soils and choose the best seeds for the future.

Lots of churches look toward their futures by making long-range plans. Some of those plans take the form of long wish lists, basing tomorrow on hopes that may not be reality or address needs. Too many of those sets of goals end up on a shelf in the church office and are never implemented after the dreaming is done. The most frequent shortcoming of many such efforts is the disconnection between identity and intention, the lack of futures sprouting from a strong and deep root system.

Second Presbyterian has planned wisely, building its future on its deepest values for the past and present. Its plan is to base its future on its identity. That approach sagely roots the future of the church in the depths of its own theology, heritage, values, and witness.

Before you read Second's identity statement, give yourself "eyes to see" several unique features about identity:

- First, most church identity statements read like bumper stickers rather than theological foundations. The following statement rests firmly and overtly on biblical and traditional beliefs.
- This identity statement is even more that a declaration of faith. It's also the anchor for planning and future programming, providing the base for implementation of ministries. The balance in the statement avoids bias and skirts attempts to make minor themes into major issues.
- The church intends to welcome broken people, help them transform their lives in Christ, and become people who minister across the Roanoke Valley.

You may wonder why this introduction even appears. These statements are here because they are unusual in the lives of most congregations. Because they are rare and foundational, they are flagged for their value and so you don't read by them without recognizing their importance.

Living Second Presbyterian's Core Identity

Since the Session approved the Identity Statement on March 24, 1999, the following statement has guided the planning and ministries of Second Presbyterian's faith and practice.

We are a church of Jesus Christ.

The one God we know as Father, Son and Holy Spirit is the God we worship and serve. Christ is the head of the church and the center of our faith and practice. We seek the guidance of God's Holy Spirit, the Living Word among us, in our corporate and individual lives.

We are a church of the Bible.

The Bible, as the written word that witnesses to the Living Word, is our guide for faith and practice. We are committed to bringing the best of biblical scholarship to bear upon our understanding of scripture, prayerfully seeking the guidance of the Holy Spirit in our interpretation.

We are a Presbyterian church.

Our theology is catholic in its commitment to the Triune God, reformed in its commitment to the essential tenets of Reformed faith, and representative in its polity. We belong to the Presbyterian Church, USA. The great ends of the church as defined by the denomination's Book of Order guide the church's program and mission. We seek to serve our denomination and tradition primarily through the building of our congregation as a community of faith. Our witness is to the whole of the Gospel; therefore, we do not traditionally identify with any special interest organizations with the church.

We honor tradition.

We seek to honor the historic and theological traditions of our Reformed faith. We utilize forms of worship and study that have nourished Presbyterian churches for centuries. While we are open to innovation and new directions, any change must come from the Christocentric tenets.

We are an accepting church.

Second Presbyterian honors the grace of God in Jesus Christ by accepting all those who look for a church home, no matter their economic condition, skin color, or the mistakes they make. We are a church for those who are single, married, divorced or widowed; for those who are childless, have children at home or children grown; for those who are happy or hurting; those with great need and those with great resources. We seek to be a church where children know they are valued and where the elderly know they are not forgotten. As far as possible, we wish to honor diversity of opinion within our membership. At Second Presbyterian, we accept each other for who we are, and who we will become, by God's grace.

We are committed to transforming lives.

Our prayer is to be God's instrument in reaching and transforming lives, helping members and visitors grow in their Christian faith. We seek to help each other understand what it means to be obedient to the ordination of our baptism. Numerical growth is accepted as a happy consequence of being a healthy church community.

We are a high commitment church.

We understand that we are who we are through the commitments we keep. We understand that in this chapter of American life, high commitment churches are growing as they make a difference in people's lives, and low commitment churches are struggling to survive. We invite strong commitment to Christ and the work of Christ's church by providing ministries through which people may grow in grace and know the joy of serving our Lord. We promote healthy stewardship of resources which includes proportionate giving of one's time, energy, and money to the life of the church as an expression of one's faith.

We are a servant church.

We understand that God blesses us in order to be a blessing. We serve and strengthen members in order to enable them to serve the world, proclaiming the good news of Jesus Christ through word and deed. The Roanoke Valley looks to Second Presbyterian to be a servant community, and we accept that responsibility. We seek to offer and support programs that benefit others outside our immediate church family. We also accept a responsibility to address needs nationally and internationally through missions both Presbyterian and ecumenical.

We are a metropolitan church.

Members of Second Presbyterian come from all over the Roanoke Valley. We will continue to be a church that attracts members because of who we are and what we offer rather than where we are located.

Yes or No, Not Maybe

Identity statements provide two key leadership functions. They remind us who we are and how we got this way. They also give leaders a framework for decisions, for a clear "yes" and "no" (Mt. 5:37).

When a church defines who it is, then its leaders have a foundation for saying "yes" to opportunities and advantages as well as "no" to shortcuts and temptations. Perennial leaders know that to say "yes" to the few right things, you usually have to say "no" to an array of wrong things.

Saying "no" is difficult for many of us. "No" may be the most powerful word in our language. It's potentially the most destructive word, too. For those basic reasons, perennial leaders develop a deft touch for saying "no." "No" triggers guilt, feels awkward, may embarrass us, and sometimes puts our relationships at risk. For some of us, "no" is almost impossible to utter. We choke on the word. Since "no" is a tough word for congregational leaders to use, an identity statement becomes a necessary toehold for discernment for our decisions and a balance point between the immediate decision and the longer-term implementation.

Our world offers so much information, creates so many choices, and raises expectations so high that "no" decisions become even more difficult to sort out and to say. Ironically, a clear "yes" or "no" not only clarifies directions for churches, if offered without "attitude," it may preserve and even strengthen relationships for the future. The art of the positive "no" is a basic craft for perennial leaders.[11] Second Presbyterian has practiced the power of a clear "yes" or "no."

A Community of "We"

Second is a robust community of faith, a family with a common cluster of beliefs, a community of "we." Like all cohesive communities, Second Presbyterian's sense of "we" is most obvious at the intersection of relationships and interests.[12] Perennial congregations such as Second stand at the center of a community movement in contemporary America. The nation's service sector is growing rapidly.

About one million not-for-profits operate in the United States, not including nearly 400,000 Protestant churches and many other kinds of congregations and religious organizations.

Congregations are generous givers to human entrepreneurship. Eighty percent of charitable giving—roughly $140 billion—comes from individuals, and a majority of individual gifts are made to and through congregations and religious organizations.[13]

Over more than a century of effective ministry and community building, Second Presbyterian has developed a wealth of resources. Secular scientists identify four kinds of capital, four resources beyond money:

- human capital, or the resource of members
- social capital, or the resource of belonging
- intellectual capital, or the resource of knowledge
- wisdom capital, or that common ground resource of values that sustain communities

One leadership expert describes wisdom capital in ways that remind churches of their unique resource in traditional values:

Wisdom capital is not dispensed by any treasury. It is…handed down through stories retold from age to age… It is stored in texts like the Bible… It is reflected powerfully in the founding documents of American democracy… It includes codes like the Hippocratic Oath that have stood the test of time and still make claims that are respected.[14]

Second, in unusual fashion, knows and celebrates its heritage while anticipating its future. Most congregations simply "age." They mark the passage of time and are proud of their pasts. By using the collective wisdom of the Second Presbyterian community, the church invites itself to "sage" rather than just age. Second's members find ways to tap and use this precious resource. They become stewards of the accumulated spiritual wisdom of the faith community. They practice "sage-ing"[15] about their tomorrows.

Planning to Plan

When Second Presbyterian launched its turn-of-the-century planning process, it devoted three months to this congregational discernment effort. The design was arranged to hear from all its members and to increase the sense of ownership for the eventual plan. Two primary means—focus groups and data gathering by means of questionnaires—were used. Two members lent their specialized business abilities to the success of the process. Kathy Stockburger used her consulting background to train the focus group leaders, and Frank Martin used his marketing expertise to organize the mass of data into an understandable presentation and to present the collected body of information clearly. When consensus was reached, the plan was written; and implementation began immediately. Committees and ministry groups took responsibility for elements of the plan that applied to their congregational assignments. They now report annually to the Executive Committee of the Session on the progress they've made during the current year and the next needs they intend to address. The church moved, and continues to move, from identity to intentionality.

Mapping Unknown Territory

After the self-defining and planning processes are completed, how does a congregation move toward its future? Several principles for the unfolding of the future by means of the "long range plan" are already at work in Second:

- Change happens from the center and in ways that honor and maintain the congregation's core identity. Intention builds on identity.
- Leaders are developed within the membership.
- Artifacts and visual materials are displayed visibly to remind members and guests of basic identity or "how we got this way."
- Resources are stewarded by principles and through uses that lead the church forward. Dollars are aligned with dreams.

Now and Later

Second's long range plan points to basic intentions for immediate change. Broadly speaking, the church wants to be known for its:

- bold proclamation of the good news of Jesus Christ
- high standards of quality in all programs
- excellence in the time-honored tradition of worship and music
- strong program of Christian education
- support of missions, local and abroad, with both volunteers and funds
- ministries in the immediate neighborhood, the Roanoke area, the nation, and the world
- ministry to all age groups
- high commitment of its members
- unified spirit that allows diverse opinions
- resources for the community
- clearly defined, growing endowment

To be known as a church that produces such an array of stellar ministries would be more than enough for most congregations. But, Second is already carrying through with its long-term plans.

Cultivating a Vigorous Future

The "Long Range Plan for 2001 and Beyond" spotlights a number of ministries and missions for the congregation to emphasize. The Session has used a limited term task force model to focus on needs and implement concrete advances. Infrastructure needs have been addressed, and ministry options are in the spotlight now.

Strengthening the Infrastructure

The *Finance Task Force* gave endowment funds and their relation to the Strategic Plan priority attention.

The Finance Task Force looked at the various endowment funds, explored their basic purposes, considered how they might be used strategically, and focused on applications five years out. Around the turn of the current century, the Session had already instructed that all gifts be available to be spent annually rather than being saved or reinvested. Then, this study looked even more strategically at the use of resources.

Like many church endowments, the *Second Presbyterian Church Fund*, begun in 1978, was intended largely to provide a safety net for capital improvements, property emergencies, or financial decline. These ends honor the original donors' gifts and intentions. However, the Fund isn't limited to these uses only. The use of collected funds is a basic example of how a congregation's identity informs and shapes its ministry intentions. Building on the 1999 Sessional Statement of Identity, the church intends to preserve its strong physical presence in historic Old Southwest Roanoke and to expand its mission of blessing its immediate and larger community. Available monies from this more than two million dollar body of resources will be spent annually in well-planned ways. The directors of the Fund now entertain requests for mission and benevolences purposes. To date, nearly a million dollars have been made available from the Second Fund, making possible purchases of adjoining properties, replacing a boiler and kitchen equipment, funding for playground equipment, and a variety of other uses.

The *Kittye Susan Trent Fund*, with its nearly two million dollar corpus from the estate of John Trent in honor of his daughter, underwrites programs to advanced Christian education at Second and in the larger church. This gift provides seminars, speakers, and scholarships. A seminar for new ministers is being designed with Union Theological Seminary and Presbyterian School of Christian Education staff.

Second Presbyterian also has a cluster of smaller funds, totaling nearly an additional half million dollars. For example, several endowments—

the *H. Spencer Edmunds' Fund for Distinguished Preaching and Teaching*, offering lectures by theologians of note to the community annually; the *Hollingsworth Fund*, providing scholarships at Union Theological Seminary; the *William R. Klein Continuing Education Endowment Fund*, underwriting ongoing training of church staffers; the *Ed and Edith Johnson Memorial Fund*, offering scholarships for collegians and seminarians; the *Organ and Music Fund*, providing for the maintenance of the pipe organ and for musical events; the *Maintenance Accrual Fund*, filling gaps for unbudgeted repairs and equipment; and the *Columbarium Perpetual Care Fund*, furnishing care for and assuring the future of the William R. Klein Columbarium—are all occasions of stewardship. These resources enrich the ministry of the congregation.

The *Facilities and Operations Task Force* went second in implementing long-range plans. This committee took a five-month look at the broad range of infrastructure needs—food service, maintenance and repairs, facilities use, staff costs and benefits, office costs, and communications. These basic functions of church operations undergird ministries but are mostly invisible as long as they work well. This committee put together a plan to keep infrastructure strong and unobtrusive.

Enriching Ministries

The **Christian Education Task Force** completed their report and plans in 2007. They have thought creatively and projected some helpful programs and use of facilities.

The **Congregational Life Task Force,** dealing with members and missions, is continuing its work still.

Strengthening Outreach

Second has a history of mission work in its neighborhood, in the Roanoke Valley, and overseas. It has helped plant new churches locally and supported foreign missionaries. Currently, Second's local outreach includes such ministries as the Roanoke Valley Jail Ministry, the West End Center's programs for youth, the Presbyterian Community Center, the Roanoke Area Ministries and their shelter and emergency assistance for homeless and at-risk persons, Turning Point's shelter for abused women, Interfaith Hospitality for families at risk of homelessness, the Pastoral Counseling Center, and Summer Enrichment's day camp program for inner city boys and girls. Additionally, the church has adopted the Highland Park Elementary School in their own neighborhood and fulfills the functions normally provided by a PTA.

A bit farther from home, Second is involved with the Navajo Indians and the rural poor of Western Arizona, the Beth-El Mission in Florida, the Medical Benevolence Foundation, and multiple mission trips to the Gulf Coast in response to Hurricane Katrina.

Overseas, the church has an array of commitments. The "Bibles and Bricks" project at San Juan de la Maguana in the Dominican Republic is a good example of Second's mission outreach. Sharing the love and grace of Christ, Second's volunteer missionaries will spend a week in another culture after careful preparation for the experience. This project will involve thirty active participants at Second who will either conduct Vacation Bible School or help with a construction project at schools in impoverished areas or do both.

The Dominican Republic represents a sustained, five-year effort at mission outreach by Second. The church sends teams twice each year, alternating medical missions and construction in the winter with Bible teaching and construction in the summer. Roanoke's hospitals and pharmacies cooperate in the medical projects, providing personnel and medicines. A clinic is staffed, and medical care is offered in the barrio as well. Second's teams are roughly one-half church members and one-half skilled volunteers from the Roanoke community. Second's on-site partner is Solid Rock Missions, a ministry begun by Mennonites. The church subsidizes the cost of this outreach for its members who need assistance.

Examined in its larger context, the outreach to the Dominican Republic through "Bibles and Bricks" and medical services represents stewardship of the unique gifts of Second Presbyterian Church. Seen in the context of the larger tradition, Second has an emphasis on education and the proclamation of the Gospel. Seen locally, Second serves Roanoke directly and as a vehicle to leaven the world. The congregation's unique strengths in medicine and construction serve two functions: to link to the emerging identity of Roanoke as a future medical and residential community and to transform the wider world now.

Second Presbyterian in Roanoke, Virginia, seems to be getting younger. It has energy and a description of the congregation it will become. Its "second century" has the promise of bringing Christian leavening to the Roanoke Valley and light to the wider world.

Leading Futuristic Perennials

By definition, perennial plants look to their futures. They expect another season. The same characteristic is natural to perennial congregations, such as Second Presbyterian, and to their leaders as well.

- Perennial leaders know the future of living communities is directly linked to their DNA and root systems. They stay true to their identities. That's not to say that futuristic perennials don't do new things. They recognize that novel initiatives grow out of established sources of health.
- Perennial congregations bring new members aboard by orienting them to the deeper themes of history and stories of the past and

present. They use heritage to project their strengths into the future.

- Perennial leaders will likely do their planning during the "off-season." Congregations such as Second are rarely dormant. Consequently, their leaders have to build in breathing spaces and invest in their own growth. These "breaks" can give time and distance from day-to-day routine and stimulate vision about the future. The reason to use periods of relative dormancy for preparation is plain: the growing season is for production.
- Perennial leaders are adept at challenge-response problem solving. Second Presbyterian has had little conflict or contention over its life. Debate is common, especially given the strength of their lay leaders and ministers. But those differences have been faced, discussed, and resolved without sides being formed or opposition becoming entrenched. Community and cooperation are valued more than competition.
- Perennial leaders move abstractions to concreteness. Second has a good way of moving forward with specificity. The successful "A Truck for Bill" effort made a mission project to help a truck farmer in northern Brazil personal and visual. There was a concrete object—a truck—and a specific face—Bill. Gifts were broken down in bite-size hunks so a tire or an engine, depending on the resources of the donor, could be given. The "Bibles and Bricks" project also demonstrates this same ability to make faith real and substantial.

The future is always abstract, because it hasn't unfolded into reality yet. In implementing their strategic plan, Second Presbyterian brought its dollars into alignment with its dreams early on. In the practical words of Jesus, "For where your treasure is, there your heart will be also" (Mt. 6:21). Second Presbyterian makes faith attractive and visible. That's a powerful witness for the future.

9

Perennial Lessons for Leaders

What's the secret? How do some churches grow perennially? From our seven church profiles, we see:

- patterns of stable, but not ingrown, long-term leadership from both lay leaders and clergy
- consistent emphasis on production and reproduction
- pastors with strong but not hungry egos
- substantial theology taught, preached, and modeled
- innovations growing out of local needs rather than fads
- diversity of ages, faith stages, family styles, and religious backgrounds
- change that's true to the congregation's DNA
- low levels of conflict in which differences are challenges, not competitions

Simply stated, perennial churches grow and sustain vitality over 25–30 years or longer because they intend to thrive rather than merely survive. They think longer-term. They do more than count nickels and noses and fret about next Sunday. Perennial churches set out to grow Christian disciples, and they do just that.

Perennial leaders patiently hang in there. One of the themes in the seven churches we profiled is the stability of their leaders over time. Just to take one fact about three examples—the current pastoral tenures of Mission Baptist, Second Baptist, and St. Mark's of Burlington, N.C., average more than three and one-half decades. That's remarkable. But, the continuity isn't just staying power; it's transformational continuity. In the long-term, the faithful service of lay leaders may be even more of a key. Long-term vitality reflects long-term continuity and strength among a congregation's leaders.

Thriving Perennially

Perennial churches thrive by intention and by nature. From a leadership viewpoint, they:

- major on basic ministries and stay focused
- grow roots before shoots and remain rooted
- rise from the dead and show resilience
- enjoy living in "mixed meadows" amid diversity
- draw strength and flexibility from deep theology
- bloom across three seasons and sustain productivity
- keep an eye on the horizon and live futuristically

These seven actions are in range for leaders who hope to grow their congregations perennially.

Planting Perennial Principles: Master Lessons from Perennial Leaders

Our cluster of seven perennial churches have told their stories, revealed their strengths, and pointed us toward some longer-term leadership principles. While each church profile was organized around a single perennial characteristic, the leadership principles fold into all the others and should be understood as a mosaic of mind set, attitudes, and actions. Take them as a whole, since the seven characteristics of perennials are interwoven in nature.

Some of the following lessons may seem counterintuitive. That should be no surprise to us. The very idea of long-term church growth runs contrary to the mainstream of America's microwave culture anyway. Plus, it's not the emphasis of most church growth experts' advice either. So, read thoughtfully, and be willing to relearn some basic assumptions about congregational leadership.

Perennial Principle #1: Leaders Stand on Deep Theological Foundations and the Central Designs of God

Mission Church and Ronnie Ray stick to basics. When Mission chose its basic disciple-making focus, it discovered the elegance of core beliefs. The simplicity and power of these beliefs are theological, not organizational or psychological or sociological. Doing ministry and leading from theological foundations provides a compass pointing to "true north" for the future and builds on the patterns of God's creation. Making disciples is the DNA of Mission, and, from a perennial perspective, is the heart of the Gardener's design. Perennial leaders rely on and remain in the center of Jesus' teachings.

One of the common marks of the seven pastors in our perennial profiles has to do with ego strength. Each of the seven has a sturdy ego but not a big or "hungry" ego. These leaders focus on issues of faith without attention to self-aggrandizement. Standing solidly and confidently on core issues of faith is one secret to staying perennially grounded. None of us is apt to be a better leader than we are a person. Leadership, at its deepest level, is more about being than doing. In some important ways, this affirmation turns much of the leadership literature on its ear.[1]

- First, the bulk of advice to leaders has focused on the most visible "what you do" aspect of leadership. Commonly, this counsel spotlights a specific list of outcomes or behaviors or traits. This school of thought boils leadership down to actions.
- Second, a smaller part of leadership material deals with a fairly visible "how you go about doing what you do" element of leadership. This approach highlights leadership processes, a more recent theme in leadership studies and research. Here, leadership is about focus, flow, and process.
- The third element of leadership, mostly invisible and the most recent to be emphasized in leadership studies, may have the most to do with perennial growth and sustainability. "Who you are" forms both what we do as leaders and the ways we do those things. The key is the sources we operate from, the identity issues that reveal our inner condition—our anchors in life's storms. That takes us back to the deep things of God, the foundation of perennial leadership.

Perennial Principle #2: Leaders Understand, Respect, and Extend Congregational DNA

Second Baptist Church of Richmond, Ray Spence, and other perennial churches' leaders look for ways to expand the historically innate strengths of their congregations. They recognize that DNA is destiny and can only be altered at considerable peril. For instance, Second Baptist Church began as a lay-led congregation and to this day is staffed leanly to make the most of its laity's strengths. Second's heritage of lay leadership, the key practice from Second's DNA, is apt to live on into the future. That emphasis would be virtually impossible to alter without splitting the church in multiple directions.

Some pastoral leadership experts would call a lay-led church a weak or easily manipulated congregation. Nothing could be further from the truth for Second Baptist of Richmond. It's a church where strength calls to strength. When a pastor with nearly half a century in service and some of the key business leaders in the capitol region (who are also church leaders) meet, there's lots of horsepower in the room. They recognize that maturity calls for cooperation rather than competition, and they build on each other's strengths. It's in their DNA.

Living things naturally resist alien materials, fighting them to the death. Remember that I reported that I was donor for my brother's bone marrow transplant? After my marrow was transplanted into his body, he predictably developed graft-versus-host disease. (My donated bone marrow was closely matched with his marrow—as ideally matched as if we were identical twins. Theoretically, our match was perfect.) This natural rejection reaction created an epic struggle by the immune system to reject genetic materials that weren't original to my brother. The other side of the war was the medical community's efforts to suppress the immune system enough to let the body accept my donated bone marrow. The transplant eventually "took," but my brother's immune system was so weakened that he died of an abscessed tooth a few months later. DNA is altered at a high price, at great risk, and as a final option.

Does that mean leaders never attempt to change their congregations? Not at all. Change is always happening naturally, and some change may need a catalyst. Since life and death are on the line when core DNA is breached, congregational leaders need to be sure beyond a shadow of a doubt that the changes they're attempting are necessary to confront demonic forces. Perennial leaders do an honest gut check to be sure they aren't merely comforting their own biases and blind spots in attempted changes. As I mentioned earlier, one pastor explained that he had to run off seven hundred members to save his church. What was he saving them from? If Satan was in charge of that church, then leaders face the evil directly and take the risks. If the pastor was trying to make the congregation over in his own image, God forgive him. Destroying a congregation for human motives or preferences doesn't advance the kingdom of God and isn't a perennial strategy.

Perennial Principle #3: Leaders Remain Steadfast, Patient, and Never Give Up

The story of St. Mark's United Methodist Church is a tale of unusual patience and steadiness in the face of adversity. In our world of instant gratification, neither patience nor steadfastness are valued or taught. St. Mark's and its leaders demonstrate that roller coaster rides from a good beginning to a near-death experience to new life and health are part and parcel of the biblical message of death and resurrection.

The Old Testament uses a powerful word and idea about steadfastness. The word is *chesed*, or the persistent, determined, almost stubborn covenant love of God. Always understood within the context of God's covenant with Israel, *chesed* holds up the sure, everlasting, and unshakeable love of God. The word reminds us that covenants are always two-sided promises. The Old Testament "covenant can never be finally and completely broken. It takes two to make a covenant, and it takes two to break it."[2] God has not stopped loving us. Maybe this steadfastness of God is part of what motivated and undergirded the remnant at St. Mark's United Methodist as they looked with assurance for a new future in ministry.

Steadfastness isn't just finding a routine or rut and settling mindlessly into it. Ruts are our adult versions of the Peanuts' cartoon character Linus's security blanket. Churches are notorious for creating patterns and then defending them as if the Gospel itself is at stake. It's likely the rut we now love was once a route that earlier took us on an important journey. If it has now outlived its usefulness, it can and must be replaced with other resources. It's always timely for persons of faith to try something new, to risk learning from mistakes again, and to concentrate more on the future than the past. Why? Because God is always ahead of us, blazing trails, forgiving and moving us beyond our sins, and holding eternity in his hands.

Perennial Principle #4: Leaders Value and Enrich Diversity

The Twelve who were Jesus' closest followers were a varied group. When the church was born in Acts 2, diversity was obvious. In the central passage of the Holy Spirit filling the believers (Acts 2:1–12), nearly twenty different language and ethnic groups are mentioned. That's likely just a "for example" listing that's intended to be more illustrative of the array of persons in the gathering that a fully complete record. The point is obvious. God's saving power is for all who believe and follow. Bon Air and the other perennial congregations in this study have been good stewards of the Gospel, both its message and its reach. Diversity has been and remains basic to Bon Air's life and ministry.

Bon Air and Travis Collins are clear examples of the appreciation of diversity. Bon Air lives in a mixed meadow where interaction with its community and its world are constant dynamics. The composition of the church's membership and its staff reflect their ministry milieu. The church looks like its community most of the time, and the church looks at its community all the time. Rather than expecting its ministry setting to mirror the church, Bon Air takes a missionary stance and bridges the diversity of its region.

Mixed meadows are challenges because of their complexity. Generally, perennial leaders don't go it alone or operate like Lone Rangers. They rely on second opinions from their fellow ministry staffers and on third opinions from thinking partners.[3] In our super-charged, instantly changing world, leaders cultivate advisory networks of persons who can think across boundaries and challenge mental models, paradigms, and worldviews. Perennial leaders know their perspective or opinion is not the only reality. They use sounding boards to raise questions, evaluate risks, and face uncertainties. Perennial leaders recognize that executive-level leaders often have more autonomy and less unbiased information than anyone else. They admit the half-life of expertise knowledge is shorter than ever before in human history.

We live in a practitioner era. Leaders learn from the success of other leaders. Best practices are shared in popular peer networks. The flaw in this pattern is that leaders may rely too much for their ideas and strategies on persons who are barely more able than they are. One secular commentator describes this approach as responsible for building "companies of midgets."[4] Diversity of opinion is necessary to lead diverse communities of faith.

Today's best leaders know it takes a flexible mind to unlearn old lessons and to learn diverse new ones. Perennial leaders, in particular, invite their convictions to be leavened by convictions that don't take one's own generation's preferences, denomination heritage, and national assumptions as givens. Return to Acts 2 and think about how the Resurrection and Pentecost turned the fledgling church's world on its ear. In the next thirty years, the Holy Spirit energized believers to plant congregations in varied corners and cultures of the known world.

Perennial Principle #5: Leaders Bridge Differences by Committing to Larger Truth

The key to Brandermill's ability to build on and move beyond the unique doctrinal challenges of Presbyterian and Methodist theologies demonstrates a way mixed congregations can function flexibly and manage polarities without major conflict. Rather than debating denominational distinctions, they dug deeper and found the larger, overarching theological foundation in Christian belief that bridged both perspectives. This commitment allows Brandermill to live in the murky middle of our world more effectively than many other congregations do.

Brandermill and Gordon Mapes are forced to think and act more flexibly than most churches and church leaders. The congregation is a union church of two denominations. It ministers in a diverse, high-expectation community. It rotates pastors between its affiliate denominations every eight years. That dynamism runs counter to the general human tendency of being creatures of habit. We tend to dampen our anxiety by "nest making," repeating patterns of behavior predictably. Most congregations fall into ruts quickly and defend those ruts fiercely. Have you ever heard about the warning on the banner across the western end of Main Street in St. Joseph, Missouri, for the wagon trains hurrying to the Gold Rush? It advised the pioneers, "Choose your rut carefully. You may be in it all the way to California." That's wise counsel for travelers and especially for leaders of perennial churches.

One of the marks of the seven churches profiled here is that they dealt with differences directly and promptly. They faced polarities squarely and kept differences from becoming large or overblown. It takes a clear mind and a crisp belief system to identify differences, respond to them proportionately, and handle them quickly. Max De Pree's classic description of leadership values was right. He said, "The first responsibility of a leader is to define reality."[5] Truth seeing and truth telling are basic features of perennial congregations and their leaders.

Perennial Principle #6: Leaders Focus on Production and Reproduction

Bob Disher and St. Mark's Church in Burlington, N.C., concentrate on reaching seekers for God and forming them in Christlikeness. They bloom across three growing seasons and structure their ministry calendar around those three seasons. The members and staff of St. Mark's show some of the same intoxication for their productive congregational ministries that theologian-gardener Terry Hershey describes as he counsels others on how to do perennial gardening. He enthuses:

"There's always room for one more plant," is my best advice… The preacher in me is in full gear…you can't really make a mistake in the garden. Honestly, if you don't like the way something turns out, you can always move it in the fall or early spring. That's part of the fun, and the wonder… "Experimenting," I exhort, spurred on by the choir in my mind, "that's gardening at its best."[6]

The intoxication of growing disciples of Christ is a heady brew that fits productive perennial churches like a hand in a glove. That attitude opens the door to the "art of possibility."[7] St. Mark's Church is always evaluating its effectiveness so it can use its "juice"[8] to discern and invent its next generation of ministries.

Perennial Principle #7: Leaders Cultivate Future Intention from Identity

George Anderson and the leaders of Second Presbyterian know who they are in Christ. That crisp sense of identity provides a compass to point them toward "true north." The future of this anchor congregation in the Roanoke Valley continues to flow from its basic identity.

Congregations and their leaders anchor themselves in self-identity. Their clarity about who they are provides a "signature presence"[9] to them. Family systems' experts describe this process of self-definition within life's most precious relationships and ministries clearly:

Defining a self means identifying the beliefs, values, commitments, and life principles on which we will base our lives. These determine how we will or won't behave in every circumstance of life, particularly with our closest relationships. To the extent we do this, these core commitments become a part of our *solid self*, the part of self that we do not negotiate away in our relationships.[10]

The Bible speaks of this deep aspect of personality as "heart." Richardson notes,

> Our hearts are shaped first of all in our families. We come by our strengths and our problems of the heart honestly. Our experience within that emotional system is where we first begin to create a sense of self and to determine how we will and won't behave.[11]

Second Presbyterian has developed a solid sense of self over its long history of stable leadership and ministry. That identity will continue to orient it for its tomorrows. Like Roanoke, as it transitions to a medical services center, communities of faith have a myriad of new faith challenges to face.

1. For the first time in the history of the human race, we have a majority urban world. Currently, more than 140 cities around the world have a million or more citizens in their populations. New religious fervor and poverty are both expanding dynamics in global urbanization. Fortunately, the Christian faith has the model of Paul's urban mission initiatives from the book of Acts for guidance. An element of identity can guide our intention to reach the world's cities.
2. Also for the first time, six generations are alive on earth simultaneously. For the first time, a generation of human beings is older than 85, so we can now fully profile our older generation's ministry needs. If congregations are families, "members of God's household" (Eph. 2:19), we must now become even more multi-generational, "full family" churches. Our historic identity can guide our future intentions.

An Advanced Leader Lab—What Perennial Leaders Believe and Do Deliberately

You've seen how seven selected congregations have thrived season after season. Are you ready to challenge yourself to be or become an organic, perennial leader? Several coaching consultations follow for you to consider to take you deeper into perennial leadership.

Perennial Leaders Cultivate Long-Term Life

Perennial congregations have unique challenges in leadership. Leaders of perennial churches concentrate on cultivating and reaping. Like most gardeners, they mostly seed, feed, and weed. They seed new ministries. They feed core ministries for growth and harvest. They weed out competing distractions to keep the focus on primary ministries.

The reason perennial leaders cultivate so relentlessly is simple: they are passionate about the promise of multiple harvests over many seasons. They know they will not find shortcuts to successful harvests. They realize perennials require more care than annuals. But, the payoff is long-term health, growth, and reproduction.

Perennial plants have an implied future, but no ironclad guarantees. In the midst of cultivating and harvesting, perennial gardeners stay alert for opportunities to plant and replant. For instance, bulb-based perennials and ornamental grasses are two natural examples of plants that overgrow, crowd themselves, and begin to compete with themselves. These plants need to be divided and replanted where they have enough room to flourish. It's the only way these perennials will have long-term vitality.

In other situations, healthy plants turn out to simply be planted in the wrong place. In those cases, flowers, grasses, and trees are repositioned for their health and for the good of the landscape. Some experienced gardeners are willing to move perennials up to three times to find the right place for each plant. The redesign of gardens helps balance and blend varieties of colors, textures, and heights of plants for beauty and hardiness.

While perennials grow season after season, they don't live forever. Faced with that reality, perennials produce and reproduce. For example, trees, our oldest perennials, die. But they hedge their bets along the way. Healthy, mature oaks produce a half million acorns each year. Perennials produce the seeds of their own construction. Perennial congregations find ways to morph into new fields and formats. Planting and cultivating lead to harvesting.

Perennial Leaders Find Stories of Hope and Tell Them

Perennial plants have continuity built in. They have a future. They will grow across seasons. With no foolproof guarantees, churches likewise expect futures and have an appreciation of "next." Leaders of perennial congregations keep an eye on the future and cultivate different time perspectives. They realize that communities frame time distinctively and have an innate sense of "next." An approach called "presencing," a blending of the words *presence* and *sensing,* helps leaders learn from the future as it unfolds rather than depending solely on the past.[12]

Perennial leaders are story listeners and storytellers. Three common future stories are available for mapping the arcs or trajectories of hopeful timeframes.[13] In culture and literature, the three generic plot lines are clearly defined: win-lose, challenge-response, and mature-move. Communities, including faith communities, generally gravitate to one of these stories and develop their own folk wisdom about the future.

Congregations' basic stories of the future shape those futures whether they recognize it or not, or whether leaders recognize that fact.

Clues to which story predominates in a faith community are the words and images congregations use. Their language is full of shorthand descriptions of these three stories, if we have ears to hear them. Faith stories announce our meaning-packed memories. Hope in one form or another is common content in these testimonies. What hints or signs of distinctive future stories do you hear in your congregation? Here's a simple listening guide.

Win-Lose Stories

"Win-lose stories" have shorter timeframes. These plots describe the perception of a critical point, are more impatient about confronting issues, and tend to be more fatalistic. Win-lose stories are typically reaction plots.   Similar to the poker player who's ready to risk it all, these stories are "all in."

- We put "all our eggs in one basket."
- We draw "a line in the sand."
- We "go for broke" and believe it's "now or never."
- We're down to "the last straw."
- We announce testily that "it's about time."

Win-lose stories flourish in war, sports, conspiracies, churches birthed in conflict, and on the extreme fringes of religions and ideologies. In the American experience, the Civil War is our quintessential win-lose plot line. Do you hear win-lose themes in you or in your congregation's story?

Challenge-Response Stories

"Challenge-response stories" have timeframes of intermediate length. These plot lines speak of tipping points, hope for and work toward better outcomes, and live fairly realistically. They often take a "what if?" approach to problems and explore both-and options. Challenge-response stories are resolution plots.

- We say that "necessity is the mother of invention."
- We "bite off more than we can chew."
- We observe that "a kite rises against the wind."
- We admit "it's easier said than done."
- We hope "the grass is greener on the other side of the fence."
- We admit that we "can't take it with us" when we die—but we still look for ways to do so.
- We try, "when life gives us lemons, to make lemonade."

Challenge-response stories thrive in adventures about exploration, discovery tales, pioneer quests, and processes of invention. Some historians hold up the experience and ethos of the settling of the American West as the primary challenge-response story in the United States.[14] Are you aware of challenge-response elements in you or in your own church's story?

Mature-Move Stories

"Mature-move stories" adopt longer timeframes. These stories assume no immediate crisis, tend to be more optimistic and more systemic, and show more patience as time unfolds naturally. Mature-move stories are reproduction stories.

- We note that "only time will tell."
- We admit we only "see the tip of the iceberg."
- We take a "so far, so good" attitude.
- We plan to "turn over a new leaf."
- We hope things are "on the mend."

Mature-move stories deal with sweeps of time and are central in historical sagas, rise-and-fall records, metamorphosis narratives, and progress arcs. These stories trace the growth and/or reproduction of cultures, concepts, and ideas. Some events that opened doors and created new mythologies in America include the Louisiana Purchase, the California Gold Rush, the transcontinental railroad, and the Great Depression. Do you hear these themes in you or in the language and stories of your church?

Jesus was a great story listener and storyteller. Since each of the three plotlines has its own place and time, Jesus used all types of stories to connect with, center, and challenge people.[15] In terms of win-lose stories, he told about the rich fool who bet his life on bigger barns and lost all (Lk. 12:13–21) and about a rich man who relied on his wealth, watched beggar Lazarus waste away, and ended up in hell (Lk. 16:19–31). Jesus applied challenge-response stories when he told about a good Samaritan (Lk. 10:29–37) and the persistent friend (Lk. 11:5–8). He also used mature-move stories when he announced the moment of the Kingdom had ripened and was near (Mk. 1:15) and when he pointed out his time of public ministry hadn't fully arrived (Jn. 7:6). In fact, one story incorporated all three story types. In the parable of the prodigal son (Lk. 15:11–32), Jesus' "every man" story, he showed the waiting father mature and move, the son lost away from home respond to challenges, and the son lost at home make the homecoming a win-lose occasion for himself.

Leaders, by definition, are community members who keep an eye on horizons. One way to discover the timeframes of your community is to listen for the plot lines and observe the outcomes of these stories in your congregation's history and current behaviors. But, that's only the beginning. As a leader, your language, the stories you choose and tell, and the timeframes you spotlight shape futures. Remember that perennials assume continuity, providing a root system in the past for the next season of ministry. Perennial leaders deal in hope.

Perennial Church Leaders Provide Immune Responses

Leaders have many strategic opportunities to provide healthy immune responses to community threats, both outside and inside of the body. Just as our immune system protects our physical health and life, faith communities constantly deal with threats to their unique DNA, identity, and history, both internally and externally. Standing steadfast on core identity and rebuffing outside invaders are pivotal opportunities for community leaders to offer immune options.

Our human bodies have a network of multifaceted internal body-guards, our elaborate immune systems, to protect us from the onslaughts of invaders. One hundred trillion cells or so make up our bodies. One in every one hundred of those cells is there to protect us. That's a significant militia.

Our immunity defense is a powerful force. Immunity identifies what's "us" and "not us." Immune responses isolate and repel the "not us" from "us." It's the basic attempt of all living things to continue living. Jesus set out the issue of yes-or-no years ago, and that clarity between what fits me and what isn't me remains a basic leadership dynamic to this day (Mt. 5:37). Leaders, in part, are guards against identity theft at the most profound and basic level.

In simplest terms, here's the broad biological pattern[16] our bodies use to marshal our immune forces. It's a general map of what happens when a pathogen gets through the external barriers and invades a human body.

The Body's Immune Defense System

Phagocyte cells provide the first line of internal defense. These cells act like the sweepers in a swimming pool, patrolling, cleaning, and washing away suspicious materials. Phagocyte cells, our scavengers, also serve as the early warning system for the body and send out the 911 calls to alert the more aggressive elements of our immune system of threats.

Our first responders are "helper T cells." These lymphocyte cells serve as the front-line commanders, rushing to the site to identify the enemy. They are the immune system's reconnaissance units. If the detected invader is a legitimate threat, the helper T cells immediately call in the body's crack combat troops.

"Killer T cells" are the special operations troops of the body. These lymphocytes have a simple and lethal combat mission. They array and attack the invading threat to kill it off.

With the battle underway, "B cells" become the body's arms factory. These lymphocytes produce antibodies to finish the task of repelling the invaders. They either neutralize the pathogens or tag them for others to execute later.

With the tide of battle turned back toward health, "suppressor T cells" survey the battle front and declare "All's clear." By calling off the attack, they are the peacemakers of our immune systems.

The "sweeper" cells then take over again at this stage to clean up litter and to repair tissue damage.

The threat may be over, but it's not forgotten. After the onslaught is faced and the threat successfully rebuffed, "memory cells" circulate through the body with earlier recognition of future threats and stronger immunity against the same or similar attacks. That's the theory behind inoculation, of course.

Perennial plants don't have an "active" circulating biochemical immune system like animals. But plants are "immune," too. They have a variety of other ways to protect and defend themselves effectively. Passive physical barriers such as thick bark as well as more aggressive methods such as irritating or toxic juices to repel invaders protect host plants from other organisms' efforts to undermine health and integrity.

Most major decisions and many congregational conflicts are occasions when immune responses are needed. In our case histories, remember that most of our profiled perennial congregations faced crossroads decisions and chose to be "us" and remain true to their DNA.

Perennial Church Leaders Avoid Friendly Fire

Even with healthy immune systems, however, sometimes people and communities still don't survive. In the early 1970s, I remember walking through the Lawrence, Kansas, graveyard of the Haskell Indian Institute, one of two Bureau of Indian Affairs colleges in the United States. I was shocked that about one-half of all the graves in the cemetery marked deaths in 1918 from flu. Now, we know some reasons why those deaths may have occurred in such high numbers.

Recently, new studies have been done of the deadly Spanish flu virus that killed at least fifty million people globally in 1918 and 1919.[17] Using reverse genetics, copies of the 1918 virus's genetic blueprint have been recovered. In animal studies, the reconstituted virus triggered frantic, "storm" responses by the immune system to counteract it. The body's own defense became so accelerated and so aggressive that lungs filled up with bloody liquids, creating a pneumonia that literally drowns the body in its own fluids. Younger people were most vulnerable, perhaps because they had the strongest and most reactive immune responses to toxic attacks. The internal battle for survival was so dramatic and relentless that some people died the first day of infection, and most of the fatalities happened within a week. The virus found a way to turn bodies against themselves, triggering lethal overreactions. Current medications are more effective against most varieties of flu, but the 1918 microbe was a truly bad bug.

For all the advantages we humans derive from our immune systems, occasionally our immune systems turn on us and create a barrage of "friendly fire." Why would our natural shields turn against us and cause disease? The causes and triggers of autoimmune reactions are not always clear, but the results are. Type 1 diabetes, rheumatoid arthritis, lupus, and an array of female disorders are common examples of autoimmune diseases. In fact, women are two to three times more likely to acquire an autoimmune disorder. The reason may be the same phenomenon noted above. Women may have enhanced immune systems when compared to men.

In our cluster of seven perennial churches, internal conflict was rarely immobilizing and was usually quickly contained. They avoided friendly fire. As mentioned above, perennial congregations contain the seeds of their own construction.

Perennial Church Leaders Think and Act Seasonally

Thinking and acting with a seasonal mind set applies to all leadership initiatives. One obvious example is evaluation. Evaluating perennial congregations is a relentless season-by-season process. Each season has its own unique ministry opportunities and challenges. Raise the questions below thoughtfully for your congregation's ministries.

Evaluating "Spring" Ministries: A Season to Plant and Cultivate

1. Which of our ministries have a young, energetic, and distinctive feel?
2. Are we growing sturdy root systems for these ministries?
3. Are we cultivating and feeding these promising ministries enough?
4. Are these ministries "perennials" with longer-term productivity, or are they "annuals" that will have to be replanted each season?
5. Are we staffed and developing leaders for new, creative ministries?

Evaluating "Summer" Ministries: A Season to Grow and Produce

1. Which ministries are now strong, fruitful, and mature?
2. Are we intentionally feeding the health and vigor of these productive ministries?

3. Are we supporting our core ministries well?
4. Are we competing with our own successful ministries and canni-balizing them?
5. Are we training leaders in emerging fields and for future needs?

Evaluating "Fall" Ministries: A Season to Reap and Rest

1. Are we losing our edge in some ministries?
2. Which ministries have passed their prime and are ready to be harvested and left behind?
3. Are we assessing the yields and life cycles of new and traditional ministries accurately?
4. Which ministries are becoming more difficult to renew and/or maintain?
5. Are we staffing for smooth successions for future leadership transitions?

Evaluating "Winter" Ministries: A Season to Plan and Prepare

1. Which ministries should have our best seedbeds, most resources, and primary focus for future growth?
2. Are we doing enough research and development for our future opportunities?
3. Are we exploring new and emerging ministries deliberately?
4. Are we providing sufficient infrastructure for our future?
5. Are we actively looking for new ministry partners and future resources?
6. Is your church thinking seasonally to grow seasonally?

Perennial Leaders Speak with a Prophetic Voice

In biblical literature, prophets are dramatic voices for faithfulness to God. Prophets raise theological and moral sensibilities higher. Prophetic leaders challenge the community to move beyond complacency and to tie timeframes—past, present, and future—together. Perennial leaders do the same. They stir, stretch, and open up their congregations. As organic leaders, they challenge their congregations to claim their futures. Prophetic leaders keep the bar high.

During my much younger days, I ran track. Among other events, I ran hurdles. The low hurdles were a fairly straightforward contest—a sprint with ten hurdles at a height that allowed the runner to stride over them smoothly without losing momentum or balance. The high hurdles were an entirely different matter, at least for me. This sprint, it seemed to me as I ran, was rudely interrupted ten times by high jumps. The simple act of raising the bar to three feet made the race challenging for me, creating a helter-skelter run with ten jumps high enough to force me to gather myself and focus on every leap individually. The challenge jarred me. But that's precisely what perennial leaders do when they stretch our timeframes into the future and force us to see God moving in front of us.

Perennial Leaders Are Eternally Hopeful

Think of it. What's more an act of faith and hope than putting a seed into the ground? Gardeners and farmers may prepare seedbeds carefully, select high-quality seeds, and choose planting times deliberately. But growers know that from the moment soil is placed over the seeds until new seeds are harvested, the growing process is largely out of their hands, even with interventions such as fertilizing and watering. Only God rotates seasons, germinates seeds, sends rains, and calls the sun to shine on growing things. Growing people or plants will make mystics of leaders. There's so much that's beyond our reach, so much that we can't account for directly. Organic leaders are cultivators of hope.

Positive psychology is a recent movement in American thinking. Launched by scholars such as Martin Seligman at the University of Pennsylvania and Mihaly Csikszentmihalyi at Claremont Graduate University, this scientific approach builds on the impacts of positive emotions, character strengths, and the search for more meaning in life. From a practical standpoint, leaders deal in tomorrows, stimulating hope in persons and groups.

Like the positive psychologists, perennial leaders raise some powerful coaching questions for other leaders and congregations.[18]

- What are your signature strengths? What are those things you excel at and do easily? Christians recognize the practice of spiritual gifts in this emphasis.
- How can you use your signature strengths to do something new?
- How can you use your curiosity to stretch your contributions to others? Hope and faith help us move beyond typical comfort zones into stretch zones.
- How can you expand the habit of saying "Thank you" into the practice of paying a gratitude visit or writing a gratitude note to others who have blessed your congregation and made your life better? Cultivating an attitude of gratitude makes leaders more appreciative and encourages those who bless us as well.
- With which one of your memories would you be willing to spend an eternity? Knowing that memories spring from our meaningful life experiences, what means most to you? Leaders are meaning makers. We help communities "make sense" and leave memories.
- What acts of service give you the keenest sense of well-being?

Life is more than feeling good. From a Christian perspective, life and hope are enriched by doing God's work in good ways. Knowing that hope is a gift of God, leaders practice optimism in freelance fashion and realize it's more like living in a formless meadow than a formal Japanese garden. Leaders are content to let God create the future and concentrate on weeding and watering until the harvest.

George Anderson told me an interesting story about the triumph of hope related to his call to Second Presbyterian. He was pastor of a church in Jackson, Mississippi, when half of Second's search committee visited him. The relationship clicked immediately. But a few weeks later, when the other half of the committee came to see him, hardly anything went smoothly. Snow delayed their flight for hours. The hotel lost their reservations. Then, George preached a sober sermon on sin as part of a Lenten series. Nothing clicked that weekend.

So the process of examining more than 300 candidates went on and on at Second. Finally, the search process ground to a halt and began all over again with George as the only carry-over candidate. At that stage, most ministers would have bowed out of the process. But both the committee and George felt a connection they shouldn't break. George went about his work in Jackson, completing several key ministry projects. Finally, both the search committee and George reached the same conviction, and George was called to Second Presbyterian as pastor. Hope that God would bring the right pastor at the right time in the right place to Second paid dividends for the congregation and for George. Perennial leaders remain eternally optimistic that God has a plan unfolding for us.

Perennial Leaders Practice the 3 R's

In the days of traditional education, students were schooled in the 3 R's of reading, 'riting, and 'rithmatic. Perennials leaders concentrate on 3 R's as well. They spotlight rooting, reproducing, and rebounding.

- Rooting provides continuity for challenges, DNA for dreams, and staying power for eras of stretch.
- Reproducing concentrates on being productive and then replicating the production season after season.
- Rebounding comes from the resilience of perennials. With future seasons ahead, perennials have other chances.

Postscript on Perennial Leaders: Spotting Them, Growing Them

You've seen what perennial churches value and how they do their ministries. You've looked over the shoulders of their leaders, both clergy and lay, and observed their beliefs and behaviors. Now, you may be ready to identify perennial leaders for your own congregation. Or, you may want to plant some perennial seeds in your own life and ministry.

How can you spot perennial strengths in others? How can you grow yourself as a perennial leader? Here are some identifiers.

- *Perennial leaders have tri-focal vision.*
  They view God's redemptive work through three visual perspectives—past, present, and future.
- *Perennial leaders appreciate roots and heritage.*
  They don't let today's opportunities slide by. They, most importantly, think theologically and practically about what God's doing and about to do. They see God as unfolding the eternal processes of redeeming humankind.
- *Perennial leaders grow people and things.*
  They are disciplined and deliberate, growing themselves and cultivating their souls. They recognize potential in their children and friends, their pets and plants. Industrial psychologists claim having a plant in the workplace is a sign of good mental health. I became concerned about my family physician's wellness when I noticed he had two plants in my examining room—both at the point of death! For a variety of reasons, I no longer see him.
- *Perennial leaders are mature and comfortable in their own skins.*
  They are grown-ups and readily admit the universe is larger than they are. They don't assume their own spines are the axes of the earth. They speak more of God and others than themselves. They can humbly wait on God and patiently wait on others. They remember God has been redeeming his creatures and creation for eons and are grateful to be junior partners in this wondrous process. They know God's timing doesn't depend on their personal watches or calendars. Perennial leaders have an impeccable sense of timing. They recall that Jesus arrived on the scene when time had ripened and was full (Gal. 4:4). They can delay action until the moment has matured in congregations and people for God's harvest.
- *Perennial leaders remain devoted to the kingdom of God.*
  They anchor themselves in the core of Jesus' teaching, the unfolding kingdom of God. They sense where God is already at work in congregations and people, and they invest their imaginations, energies, and faith in those junctions of growth. They lead organically, planting, cultivating, and harvesting the things God germinates.

May it always be so!

Notes

Introduction: What Makes "Perennial Churches" Distincive and Rare?

[1]Jared Diamond, *Collapse: How Societies Choose to Fail or Succeed* (New York: Viking, 2004).

[2]For a basic primer in leading living communities, see Peter Senge, "Leadership in Living Organizations," in *Leading beyond the Walls,* ed. Frances Hesselbein, Marshall Goldsmith, and Iain Somerville (San Francisco: Jossey-Bass, 1999), 73–90, and Robert D. Dale, *Seeds for the Future: Growing Organic Leaders for Living Churches* (St. Louis: Lake Hickory Resources, 2005).

Chapter 1: Growing Perennially

[1]Elton Trueblood, *The Predicament of Modern Man*, 4th ed. (New York: Harper and Brothers, 1944).

[2]Howard Foltz and Ruth Ford, *Paradigm Lost: Rediscovering God's Plan for Spiritual Harvest* (Waynesboro, Ga.: Authentic Media, 2004), 23.

[3]Terry Hershey, *Soul Gardening* (Minneapolis: Augsburg Fortress Press, 2002).

[4]Jon Piper, as cited in Janine M. Benyus, *Biomimicry: Innovation Inspired by Nature* (New York: HarperCollins, 1997), 23.

[5]Jim Collins, *Good to Great and the Social Sectors* (Boulder, Colo.: Jim Collins, 2005), 4–9. This section of Collins' material focuses on defining "great."

[6]Benyus, *Biomimicry*, 25.

[7]Ibid., 35.

[8]Many pests prefer one special host species. In diverse mixes of types, pests find thriving is a challenge and often move on to more homogenous and more promising settings. See Benyus, *Biomimicry*, 26.

[9]Ibid., 33.

Chapter 2: Leading Purposive Perennials

[1]In the late 1990s, the Baptist State Convention of North Carolina commissioned an array of regional studies of North Carolina's subcultures and growth patterns in an "Our Common Future" series. The purpose of these scenarios was to establish compatible new churches and ministries across these regions. One of those studies, "The Hub," explored Charlotte and its surrounding counties and was released in April of 2000. The futurist who authored these unpublished competitive intelligence materials and perspectives is Cassidy S. Dale.

[2]Stanly County was established in 1841 when it was divided from Albemarle County. The county is named for John Stanly, a colonial era lawyer who served two terms in the U.S. House of Representatives and three terms in the North Carolina House of Representatives. He killed Richard Dobbs Spaight, a signer of the United States Constitution in a duel in 1802, leading to the outlawing of dueling in North Carolina.

[3]An informal history of Mission was prepared by Mrs. Sandy Burr covering the hundred years spanning 1876 to 1976. The timeline reaches from the early prayer meeting that grew into Mission to the calling of Ronny Russell as pastor.

[4]Ronny Russell, *Can A Church Live Again?: The Revitalization of a 21ˢᵗ Century Church* (Macon, Ga.: Smyth and Helwys, 2004), 7. Much of the information incorporated into this chapter was drawn from Ronny's book and from conversations with him.

[5]Ibid., 6–8.

[6]Willi Evans Galloway, "1 Landscape, 2 Ways," *Organic Gardening* (February-March 2007): 58–63.

[7]Craftsmen are needed by all kinds of professions, including congregations. For example, the carpenter who knows his craft understands the need to be clear and exacting about his challenges. For an interesting treatment on design craft in carpentry, see Norm Abram, *Measure Twice, Cut Once: Lessons from a Master Carpenter* ((Boston: Little, Brown and Company, 1996).

[8]Visit T-Net's Web site at www.tnetwork.com for more information on their ministry.

[9]Terry Hershey, *Soul Gardening: Cultivating the Good Life* (Minneapolis: Augsburg Press, 2000).

[10]Ronny Russell, "Beyond Jerusalem: Learning from a Decade of Disciplemaking," available at www.netresults.org/online/2007/JanFeb/disciplemakingpart1.html.

[11]For explanation of this model of community ministries and missions, see David W. Crocker, *Operation Inasmuch: Mobilizing Believers beyond the Walls of the Church* (St. Louis: Lake Hickory Resources, 2005).

[12]Ronny Russell, *Can a Church Live Again?*, 87.

[13]Ibid., 83.

[14]Ibid., 51–52.

[15]Ibid., 131.

[16]These qualities are listed in an e-mail from Eddie Hammett on February 5, 2007. Eddie has a long-term and catalytic relationship with Mission's lay leaders and with Ronny.

[17]David Heenan and Warren Bennis, *Co-Leaders: the Power of Great Partnerships* (New York: John Wiley and Sons, 1999).

[18]David J. Wood, "Jazz Improvisation and the Peculiar Work of Pastors," available at www.divinity.duke.edu/programs/spe/articles/200702/jazz.html. Other helpful explorations of leadership as improvisation include Max De Pree, *Leadership Jazz* (New York: Dell, 1992), and Jeremy S. Begbie, *Theology, Music, and Time* (Cambridge: Cambridge University Press, 2000).

[19]The imaginary newspaper article about Mission's future is datelined October 1, 2016 and is available from Ronny Russell.

Chapter 3: Leading Rooted Perennials

[1]Barbara Brown Taylor, *Leaving Church: A Memoir of Faith* (New York: HarperSanFrancisco, 2006), 17.

[2]The staff and members of Second Baptist Church of Richmond know and appreciate their heritage, in part from a trio of histories of the congregation by Solon B. Cousins et al., *Historical Sketches of Second Baptist Church, Richmond, Virginia* (Richmond, Va.: The Second Baptist Church, 1964); Belle Gayle Ellyson, *The History of the Second Baptist Church, Richmond, VA, 1820–1970* (Richmond, Va.: The Second Baptist Church, 1970); and John S. Moore, *The History of the Second Baptist Church, Richmond, VA, 1820–1995* (Richmond, Va.: The Second Baptist Church, 1998). I know this church informally as well as from the formal histories. When Virginia Baptists established a Young Leaders' Program in 1989, we soon looked for a nearby church to experience leadership as a living case study. Second was our choice. The Young Leaders' group spends a day at Second each January. Ray Spence, recently retired longtime pastor, would set the stage for understanding leadership in changing contexts, the staff would describe how staffs work together, and the group would get a walking tour of ministries and facilities. During the early 1990s, Ray was joined by the late Buck Street, a key layman at Second who had chaired the transition process from the downtown site to the current campus at River Road and Gaskins. Interestingly, each remembered the process differently. They didn't disagree. But they, like most witnesses to common events, had seen and experienced the move from the city to the county from different perspectives. The telling of the story, or stories, provided vital leadership lessons to novice leaders—not everyone sees the same situation in the same way. And the differences enrich the solutions. Beyond these basic histories and the annual Young Leaders' Program reports, much of the background for this chapter came from conversations with Ray Spence, Sterling Moore, and other informal exchanges with church members.

[3]Ellyson, *History of the Second Baptist Church, 1820–1970*, 99.

[4]Much of the story of this array of missionaries is chronicled in ibid., 45–53.

[5]Moore, *History of the Second Baptist Church, 1820–1995*, 49.

[6]Ellyson, *History of the Second Baptist Church, 1820–1970*, 68.

[7]Malcolm Gladwell, *The Tipping Point: How Little Things Can Make a Big Difference* (Boston: Little, Brown and Company, 2000), 9.

[8]Nelson Granade, *Lending Your Leadership: How Pastors Are Redefining Their Role in Community Life* (Herndon, Va.: Alban Institute, 2006).

[9]Richard Southern and Robert Norton, *Cracking Your Congregation's Code: Mapping Your Spiritual DNA to Create Your Future* (San Francisco: Jossey-Bass, 2001), 17.

[10]Ronald W. Richardson, *Becoming a Healthier Pastor: Family Systems Theory and the Pastor's Own Family* (Minneapolis: Fortress Press, 2005), 59.

[11]Mary Beth O'Neill, *Executive Coaching with Backbone and Heart* (San Francisco: Jossey-Bass, 2000), 120.

[12]Robert D. Dale, *Seeds for the Future: Growing Organic Leaders for Living Churches* (St. Louis: Lake Hickory Resources, 2005), 59–78.

Chapter 4: Leading Resilient Perennials

[1]The information for this chapter was largely provided from printed materials and by group and individual interviews with Pastor David Bonney, Judy Hawthorne, Harry Rast, Jane Davis, Helen Anderson, Barbara Hunt, and former pastor David Adkins. Their reviews of drafts for fact checks and interpretation were invaluable. Originally, St. Mark's as a perennial congregation was suggested to me by Franklin Gillis, formerly the superintendent of the Richmond District of the United Methodist Church.

[2]This historical statement is from St. Mark's fortieth anniversary celebration bulletin.

[3]Eventually, the parsonage would be sold by the District with the proceeds applied to a housing allowance for St. Mark's pastors. David Adkins was the first pastor of the congregation to purchase and live in his own residence.

[4]For the fuller story, see Gene Kranz, *Failure Is Not an Option: Mission Control from Mercury to Apollo 13 and Beyond* (New York: Simon and Schuster, 2000). Additionally, Jim Lovell wrote his account of the near-disaster in *Lost Moon* (New York: Pocket Books, 1994).

[5]Malcolm Gladwell, *The Tipping Point: How Little Things Can Make a Difference* (Boston: Little, Brown and Company, 2000).

[6]Peter L. Steinke, *Congregational Leadership in Anxious Times: Being Calm and Courageous No Matter What* (Herndon, Va.: Alban Institute, 2066), 73.

[7]Bernd Heinrich, *Winter World: The Ingenuity of Animal Survival* (New York: HarperCollins, 2003), 248.

[8]For more information about Art for Humanity, see www.artforhumanity.org.

[9]Pat Summit, as quoted in Oliver "Buzz" Thomas, *Ten Things Your Minister Wants to Tell You (But Can't Because He Needs the Job)* (New York: St. Martin's Press, 2007), ix.

[10]See Garry Emmons' on-line article, "The Business of Global Poverty," from April 4, 2007 in Harvard Business School's e-letter, *Working Knowledge for Business Leaders,* available at http://hbswk.hbs.edu/item/5656.html.

Chapter 5: Leading Diverse Perennials

[1]The basic historical information for this chapter is drawn from Lucien T. Hall Jr., *Bon Air Baptist Church, 1952–1982: Three Decades of Christian Fellowship.* This material was published by the church to mark its thirtieth anniversary and provides clear timelines and factual information drawn primarily from the minutes from church conferences and formal programs. Other perspectives have been provided in interviews of all of the pastors of the church and of key lay leaders, as well as reviews of drafts by congregational leaders.

[2]Woodland Heights Baptist Church, founded in 1910 at Springhill Avenue and West 31st Avenue, had established the Jahnke Road Baptist Church in 1949. As it grew, Woodland Heights developed a generous mission support reputation. It earmarked 40 percent of its 1950 and 1951 budgets for mission outreach, surveyed the Bon Air area, and voted in May of 1952 to begin a new church in Bon Air. Later, Woodland Heights would also plant the Derbyshire and Huguenot Road Baptist Churches as well. The generosity of Woodland Heights for missions grew to 43 percent of offerings in 1957. Its annual gifts to establish Bon Air ranged from $2500 in 1952 to $6000 in 1957.

[3]Janine M. Benyus, *Biomimicry: Innovation Inspired by Nature* (New York: Perennial, 1997), 26.

[4]An interview with Garry Sims on January 28, 2007, lent the basic background for this segment. Garry, who found Christ while in prison himself, literally knows prison ministry from the inside out.

[5]Frank Green, "Va. Prison Population Expected to Increase," *Richmond (Virginia) Times-Dispatch,* February 15, 2007, B8.

[6]Much of the information for this section came from an interview with Teresa McBean on January 25, 2007.

[7]For basic information about NorthStar Community's recovery ministries, visit www.northstarcommunity.com.

[8]These ideas are adapted and expanded from Dave Ferguson, "The Multi-Site Church: Some of the Strengths of This New Life Form," (1–26–07), www.christianitytoday.com/bcl/areas/vision-strategyarticles/le-2003–002–21.81.html.

[9]Mary Catherine Bateson, *Peripheral Vision* (New York: HarperCollins, 1994), 53.

[10]David Briggs, "Data Explore Role of Religion in U.S. Life," *Baptists Today* 15, no. 1 (January 2007): 28.

Chapter 6: Leading Flexible Perennials

[1]A packet of orientation materials, along with a guidebook of Brandermill Church, is given to new members. Included in that bundle of informative items is an overview of the history and organization of the congregation. This description of a union church is part of that record.

[2]Ed Briggs, "New Church Difficult to Peg," *Richmond (Virginia) Times-Dispatch,* August 6, 1977.

[3]The national United Methodist Church doesn't keep a total of its Cooperative Ecumenical Parishes, but the Virginia Annual Conference, the UMC entity to which Brandermill is connected, identifies three community churches in its jurisdiction.

[4]For the Chesterfield County Report to Citizens 2007, see www.co.chesterfield.va.us/ReporttoCitizens.

[5] This is the motto or description Brandermill uses on its promotional materials.

[6]This basic story is taken from an interview with D. Clyde Bartges on February 14, 2007, as well as from his brief statement of the early history of Brandermill Church in the welcome packet for new members, pages 19–21.

[7]Later, these same two denominations with different leaders and different resources decided not to begin a cooperative congregation when the same developer built the Woodlake community across Swift Creek Reservoir.

[8]Both Clyde and charter member Cassandra Lacey mentioned this knack in their respective interviews.

[9]From the new member's packet materials, page 23.

[10]This observation was offered by charter member Cassandra Lacey in an interview on February 19, 2007.

[11]See Barry Johnson, *Polarity Management: Identifying and Managing Unsolvable Problems* (Amherst, Mass.: HRD Press, 1996) for an approach to dealing with complex dilemmas that don't have cut-and-dried "solutions."

[12]The new member packet traces these polarities, pages 7–15.

[13]All five of Brandermill Church's pastors were interviewed individually during the second half of February 2007.

[14]Cathy Kirkland, a nurse in the Brandermill membership, provided this information in an interview on April 10, 2007. She reported that she had wanted to go on a medical missions trip before the 1997 journey to Haiti. When she went, she felt immediately at home, loved the practical care for persons who live on life's margins, and has seen her sensitivity to making her life's materials go farther increase here at home.

[15]Tom Pakurar was interviewed about this ministry on February 27, 2007.

[16]For this perspective, see an article on the death of a prominent conservationist, "Wilson Riggan Sr. Dies at Age 92," *Richmond (Virginia) Times-Dispatch,* March 14, 2007, B8.

[17]Waldo Beach, *The Christian Life* (Richmond, Va.: CLC Press, 1966), 66–77.

[18]Frederick Buechner, cited in *Horizons: Theologian Notes Impact of FTE Fellowship* 8, no. 1 (Winter 2005): 1.

[19]This is Joe's phrase from an interview on February 27, 2006.

[20]This information was supplied by Lorraine Weatherford in an interview on February 28, 2007.

[21]The basic information on stove building and Katrina response was provided by Kit Carson in an interview on March 5, 2007.

[22]Nelson Granade, *Lending Your Leadership: How Pastors Are Redefining Their Role in Community Life* (Herndon, Va.: Alban Institute, 2006), 12.

[23]Peter Senge, "Systems Citizenship: The Leadership Mandate for This Millennium," in *The Leader of the Future 2,* ed. Frances Hesselbein and Marshall Goldsmith (San Francisco: Jossey-Bass, 2006), 38.

[24]See Johnson, *Polarity Management* for a full treatment of this resource.

[25]"Play fair" is one of Robert Fulghum's "lessons" in *All I Really Need to Know I Learned in Kindergarten: Uncommon Thoughts on Common Things* (New York: Ballantine Books, 1983).

[26]Sally Helgesen, "Challenges for Leaders in the Years Ahead," in *The Leader of the Future 2,* 186.

[27]Jonathan M. Tisch with Karl Weber, *Chocolates on the Pillow Aren't Enough: Reinventing the Customer Experience* (New York: John Wiley and Sons, 2007).

[28]Chip Heath and Dan Heath, *Made to Stick: Why Some Ideas Survive and Others Die* (New York: Random House, 2007).

Chapter 7: Leading Productive Perennials

[1]The primary information for this chapter was drawn from materials about St. Mark's Church in print and on their Web site, and both individual and group interviews. The staff interviews included Eric Allred, Cindy Bailey, Ben Bishop, Ruth Bresson, Bob Disher, Steve Flint, Tim Riddle, Jarm Turner, and Scott Woody. An interview session with a group of members included Brooke Carpenter, Richard Franks, Richard and Marjorie Henderson, Eric and Jeanne Misenheimer, Dianne and Roger Setzer, and Jean and Mike Wachenfeldt.

[2]From page 7 of the February 22, 2007, revision of the guest information booklet provided visitors to St. Mark's.

[3]Kevin J. Vanhoozer, ed., *Everyday Theology: How to Read Cultural Texts and Interpret Trends* (Grand Rapids, Mich.: Baker, 2007).

[4]This anonymous poem entitled, "Slowly…," is part of a daily devotional service from the Church of the Saviour in Washington, D.C., and is available at http://www.inwardoutward.org/?p=375.

[5]Malcolm Gladwell, *The Tipping Point: How Little Things Can Make a Big Difference* (Boston: Little, Brown and Company, 2000).

[6]For a perspective that takes volunteer and not-for-profit organizations into account, see James L. Heskett, "Managing for Results in the Community of the Future," in *The Community of the Future,* ed. Frances Hesselbein, Marshall Goldsmith, Richard Beckhard, and Richard F. Schubert (San Francisco: Jossey-Bass, 1998), 139–54.

[7]Seth Godin, *The Dip: A Little Book That Teaches You When to Quit (And When to Stick)* (New York: Portfolio, 2007).

[8]Howard Foltz and Ruth Ford, *Paradigm Lost: Rediscovering God's Plan for Spiritual Harvest* (Waynesboro, Ga.: Authentic Media, 2004), 53.

Chapter 8: Leading Futuristic Perennials

[1]The best information source for the sweep of background and heritage of Second Presbyterian is the congregation's centennial history: *A 'Second' Century: The History of Second Presbyterian Church of Roanoke, Virginia 1891–1991.*

[2]The story about Second Presbyterian deliberately choosing to face the city of Roanoke was told by A. Hayden Hollingsworth, Jr., pastor from 1942–1968, to his son J. Hayden Hollingsworth who shared it with me in an interview in May of 2007.

[3]The term "Old First" is used commonly by sociologists of religion and usually applies to the earliest church of a denominational family to be established in a place. The Old First is typically characterized by stability and strength, quality and innovation in ministry, and more breadth in the make-up of the congregation than other church types.

[4]The selection of Second Presbyterian Church in Roanoke, Va., was triggered by a suggestion from Donna Hopkins Britt, pastor at Calvary Baptist Church in Roanoke. This chapter is largely based on the written history of the church as well as on interviews with

George Anderson, Paul Anderson, Phil Boggs, Gerald Carter, Carol Dalhouse, Buddy Edmunds, Hayden Hollingsworth Jr., Bill Klein, Joe Miller, Nancy Morris, Kathy Stockburger, and Bob Williams. Additionally, a conversation with members of the Fitzpatrick family–Helen, Beverly, Shirley, Broaddus, and Luann–provided helpful perspective. The videos from the 100th anniversary celebration and for recruiting new members added inside views of the church over time and currently.

⁵Chapter 6 of *A 'Second' Century* and an interview with Edmunds's son, Buddy, provided information for this section.

⁶See the profile on Edmunds in *A 'Second' Century,* 72.

⁷Chapter 7 of *A 'Second' Century* and an interview with Hollingsworth's son, Hayden Hollingsworth Jr., have provided perspective for this section.

⁸The majority of the memorial windows are dedicated to laypersons. But four of the stained-glass windows remember three of the earlier pastors–Robert Campbell Anderson (1892–1897), Arthur Rowbotham (1901–1921), and H. Spencer Edmunds (1923–1941)–and Mary Bigham, Director of Christian Education.

⁹Chapter 8 of *A 'Second' Century* and a personal interview with Bill Klein himself informed this section.

¹⁰This identity and advertising quote appears on the back of Heinz' ketchup bottles.

¹¹William L. Ury has shown us how to get to yes, how to get past no, how get to peace, and now he shows us how to use the power of a positive no. See William Ury, *The Power of a Positive No: How to Say No and Still Get to Yes* (New York: Bantam, 2007).

¹²For a discussion of community formation, see Suzanne W. Moore, "Five Building Blocks for Successful Communities," in *The Community of the Future,* ed. Frances Hesselbein, Marshall Goldsmith, Richard Beckhard, and Richard F. Schubert (San Francisco: Jossey-Bass, 1998), 230.

¹³Bob Buford, "How Boomers, Churches, and Entrepreneurs Can Transform Society," in *The Community of the Future,* 44.

¹⁴Claire L. Guadiani, "Wisdom as Capital in Prosperous Communities," in *The Community of the Future,* 60.

¹⁵Zalman Schachter-Shalomi and Ronald S. Miller, *From Age-ing to Sage-ing* (New York: Warner Books, 1995).

Chapter 9: Perennial Lessons for Leaders

¹An interesting challenge to traditional, short-view leadership theory has been issued by MIT's C. Otto Scharmer. His "U Theory" deals with a leader's blind spot, that inner place that propels us without conscious deliberation. See www.pegasuscom.com/levpoints/scharmerexcept.html for his comments from 5/22/2007.

²Norman H. Snaith, *The Distinctive Ideas of the Old Testament* (New York: Schocken Books, 1964), 112. This classic treatment of Old Testament theology clearly reminds us that God's loving nature can be relied on.

³Saj-nicole A. Joni, *The Third Opinion: How Successful Leaders Use Outside Insight to Create Superior Results* (New York: Portfolio, 2004).

⁴Ibid., 189.

⁵Max De Pree, *Leadership Is an Art* (New York: Dell, 1989), 11.

⁶Terry Hershey, *Soul Gardening: Cultivating the Good Life* (Minneapolis, Augsburg Press, 2000), 63.

⁷Rosamund Stone Zander and Benjamin Zander, *The Art of Possibility: Transforming Professional and Personal Life* (Boston: Harvard Business School Press, 2000).

⁸Evan I. Schwartz, *Juice: The Creative Fuel That Drives World-Class Inventors* (Boston: Harvard Business School Press, 2004).

⁹Mary Beth O'Neill, *Executive Coaching with Backbone and Heart: A Systems Approach to Engaging Leaders with Their Challenges* (San Francisco: Jossey-Bass, 2002), 17–40.

¹⁰Ronald W. Richardson, *Becoming a Healthier Pastor: Family Systems Theory and the Pastor's Own Family* (Minneapolis: Fortress Press, 2005), 59.

¹¹Ibid., 60.

¹²C. Otto Scharmer, *Theory U: Leading from the Future as It Emerges* (Boston: SoL, 2007).

¹³Cassidy Dale, "Rehearsing the Future: Scenario Building," in *Trajectory: Plotting a Course to Christian Futures,* ed. Robert J. Duncan Jr. (Muskogee, Okla.: Indian University Press, 2006), 98–110.

[14]The "frontier thesis" of how America's identity was forged was represented by historians such as Charles A. Beard and Frederick Jackson Turner. Perhaps the watershed statement of this viewpoint was made in Turner's 1893 paper, "The Significance of the Frontier in American History," to the American Historical Association during the Chicago World's Fair.

[15]The connect-center-challenge model of organic leadership of communities is discussed in Robert D. Dale, *Seeds for the Future: Growing Organic Leaders for Living Churches* (St. Louis: Lake Hickory Resources, 2005).

[16]Peter Jaret, "Our Immune System: The Wars Within," *National Geographic* 169, no. 6 (June 1986): 702–34. This source is dated but is written in a manner that's understandable to nonscientific readers.

[17]David Brown, "1918 Flu Virus Limited the Immune System," *Washington Post*, January 18, 2007, www.washingtonpost.com/wp-dyn/content/article/2007/10/17.

[18]D.T. Max, "Happiness 101," *The New York Times*, January 7, 2007, www.nytimes.com/2007/01/07/magazine/07happiness.t.html.